Your Brain On Porn

Your Brain On Porn

*Internet Pornography
and the
Emerging Science of Addiction*

Gary Wilson

COMMONWEALTH

First published in the UK in 2014 by
Commonweath Publishing
commonwealth-publishing.com

The information contained in this text is not intended, nor implied,
to be a substitute for professional medical advice. It is provided for
educational purposes only. Always seek the advice of your physician
or other qualified healthcare provider before starting any new
treatment or discontinuing an existing treatment. Talk with your
healthcare provider about any questions you may have regarding a
medical condition. Nothing contained in this text is intended to be
used for medical diagnosis or treatment.

ISBN 978-0-9931616-0-5

Cover design by Kieran McCann.
Typeset by Ray Davies

For A. Masquilier, whose selflessness and foresight made possible the open dialogue that continues to fuel recoveries by the thousands

Contents

Foreword

Neuroscience, the Internet and the Good Life

Professor Anthony Jack

The human mind is shaped by the intersection of two powerful forces: biology and culture. Cultural changes, in particular technological innovations, profoundly alter how we think. Yet these changes do not occur on a blank slate. The brain is a highly plastic, flexible organ. But it is also an accident of evolution, with numerous constraints. The written word, for example, has transformed our ability to understand the world, greatly accelerating changes in technology and fundamentally changing human consciousness. Yet, unlike verbal language, reading and writing do not emerge spontaneously from human sociability. Literacy only reliably arises as the product of well-organized social institutions dedicated to education.

Literacy requires training that alters the basic wiring of the brain. It takes serious work to organize neurons into a highly efficient specialized system that links visual processing to the verbal language system and manual motor outputs. Sustained and guided attention changes the structure of the brain and endows it with new powers.

The great promise of the rapidly advancing field of human neuroscience is that it can help us to understand how cultural contexts interact with the brain to create the mind - how behaviours and ways of thinking inscribe themselves inside our skulls. It gives us a new way to put human consciousness under the light of scientific understanding. Neuroscience offers guidance that can help us fulfill our potential and avoid pitfalls along the way.

But we mustn't fool ourselves that this emerging science will deliver quick and easy fixes – fixes like taking a pill, having surgery, or passing laws severely restricting what others are allowed to do. The best way to train our plastic brains to work effectively in their cultural context is through education, inquiry and contemplation, a process that takes a lot of time and patience.

The widespread availability of high-power computers, coupled with high-speed internet connectivity, has ushered in an era of technological change whose capacity to shape human consciousness is comparable to the invention of the printing press. The internet is now everywhere. It is not just in the office buildings of the most developed countries, but also, through smartphones, in the hands of individuals of all ages everywhere. Information is flowing around the world at a quantity, speed, and with a lack of barriers that represents a sea-change from the past. This revolution is changing not just the information we have access to, but the very nature of how we ask questions (we google it), and the process we use to answer them: thinking is now as much a task shared with computers as a purely brain-based activity.

In recent years there has been widespread concern about the impact of the internet on our social lives. The internet offers wonderful opportunities for people to connect in new and meaningful ways, yet it also threatens to make us socially disconnected. Many of us have hundreds of 'friends' on Facebook whom we interact with online at the cost of face-to-face interactions. Research has shown this often has a negative effect on our well-being. Technology is in danger of making us impersonal, of dampening our capacity and tendency for human connection.

Perhaps the most important example of the way that digital technology allows us to withdraw from ordinary interaction is pornography. In a healthy relationship, sex is associated with the highest levels of intimacy and trust. It is, or at least can be, the culmination and expression of our closest human connection. It not only helps to reinforce this connection, it also creates entirely new life. Evolution shaped this basic human drive to build families: sexual desire is one of our most powerful motivational forces, and has been essential to the flourishing of the human race. Yet pornography transforms that drive into a force that primarily motivates the completely solitary and unproductive activity of masturbation.

Pornography has been present since before the dawn of civilization, and can be found on the walls of cave dwellers. Yet, it has never been less social, or more pervasive. It is well known that pornography has been the single most influential economic engine that has fuelled the expansion of the internet, including internet commerce. It is accessed in massive quantities on both computers and, more recently, smartphones, not just in the USA but increasingly across the entire world.

As a result of the internet revolution, young people don't need to physically purchase pornographic content or obtain it from friends. The current cultural environment provides massive amounts of varied content that can be accessed for free and in complete privacy. Anyone with a high-speed internet connection can, if they choose, access more sexually arousing content in a few hours than the most obsessive and wealthy collector of a few decades ago could have amassed in a lifetime.

Finally, pornography represents the most important cautionary tale of how the internet can make us impersonal because of a great irony. It turns out that sex is such a personal issue that we are reluctant to speak about it in public. We don't like to say so out loud, but the internet exists in its current form because it is, in large part, a collection of technologies that make access to pornography more convenient. Pornography is shaping the private consciousness of people all over the world, probably including most of the people you know, in a way that is quantitatively and qualitatively different from the past. It is past time for that private influence to become a subject for public deliberation.

Let me take a moment to clearly state what I believe is the best approximation of the truth, on a topic where objectivity is notoriously difficult. Addiction to internet pornography is a very real phenomenon with a very real impact on well-being. It is a phenomenon which has grown exponentially in the last decade, even though it has remained largely invisible and undetected by society. Tragically, its risks continue to be ignored or actively denied by all but a few enlightened medical professionals. It is a phenomenon that is not just here to stay, but also likely to increase. It is almost certainly the cause of the widespread sexual dysfunction found in recent studies of late adolescence.[1] It is a problem that is most likely impacting you, or your loved ones, without you even being aware of it.

The core of this book comes from the blend of two things: scientific evidence and human experience. Pornography is as old as civilization, but this book provides a scientific account of why internet pornography is having a qualitatively and quantitatively different effect from most prior pornography. This scientific account is made vivid by the first hand reports of people who have been badly impacted by, and found a way to help resolve, their addiction to internet pornography. The account that you will read is solid. I am a professor in the fields of neuroscience, psychology and ethics. I have more than 20 years of education and research experience in those fields, acquired at world leading institutions in both Europe and the USA, and I actively teach and do research. Writing this foreword is an accident in my career – something I stumbled on by chance and which grabbed me when I realized its significance. I have never even met Gary Wilson, but I have paused to study his work and the academic literature carefully. I vouch for his

---

[1] See Lucia O'Sullivan et al, "Prevalence and Characteristics of Sexual Functioning among Sexually Experienced Middle to Late Adolescents", *Journal of Sexual Medicine* 2014; 11:630-641

account without hesitation. It is the most considered, thorough and accurate account of internet pornography addiction that exists at the time of writing.

Gary's account isn't the last word, and he would never pretend it is. However, it is far more insightful than accounts I have read by tenured professors at major research universities. Furthermore, unlike many of those accounts, Gary's account is very readable. To be clear, both Gary Wilson and I feel very strongly that more research is needed, into the neuroscience of this particular addiction, and into effective therapeutic responses. Nonetheless, it is already evident that pornography poses a significant threat to the emotional wellbeing of many of its users, and it would be irresponsible not to acknowledge that threat as real and pressing.

The threat that internet pornography poses can be traced to the effects it has on the reward circuitry of the brain. This reward circuitry comprises a remarkable and complex system. It learns and changes with experience, and it is sensitive to many different sorts of rewards. The central nexus of this reward circuitry is a set of subcortical structures that lie just above and behind the eyes. These structures are usually referred to collectively as the ventral striatum, and activity in these structures indexes the degree to which a stimulus or behaviour is rewarding to the individual. Some rewards are very concrete. You won't be surprised to learn that the ventral striatum fires when people eat chocolate and when they look at pictures of attractive scantily clad people. These are obvious atavistic rewards. Evolution shaped us to desire calorie rich foods and fit mates – we wouldn't be here if our ancestors hadn't been motivated to seek those things. Similarly, it isn't very surprising that cocaine activates the ventral striatum – cocaine would never have become a popular drug of abuse if it didn't.

However, the ventral striatum is not merely activated by drugs of abuse or stimuli whose associations with reward were hard wired into our brains long ago by evolution. The ventral striatum is strongly connected to and modulated by regions involved in social processing, and it is strongly triggered by rewards which depend on social context. For instance, stimuli which signal financial gains and increase in social status also activate the ventral striatum. It is very important to appreciate that the ventral striatum is not just associated with self-serving rewards, but also motivates prosocial behaviour such as charitable giving. The ventral striatum is highly sensitive to genuine empathetic social connection, including looking at a photograph of a family member, falling in love, altruistic acts, and even the simple feeling that someone has listened to you.

Great care needs to be taken when we move from talking about reward to addiction. When addiction is being discussed in a clinical context, for instance relating to substance abuse or dependency, then by definition it means a tuning of the reward system that is dysfunctional. That is, the medical phenomenon of addiction occurs when the reward system loses its balance and becomes over tuned to prefer a type of reward that is demonstrably detrimental to our wellbeing. But the mere fact the reward system of an individual has become very strongly tuned to particular type of reward does not mean any dysfunction is present. In ordinary language, we recognize this fact. We might say that a friend is addicted to exercise, addicted to nature, addicted to reading literature, or addicted to charitable service work. Such 'addictions' can certainly exist, in the sense that people can have reward systems that are very strongly tuned to the rewards associated with these activities. Provided the tuning is not so strong that other important behaviours are completely displaced, these 'addictions' are far more likely to be healthy and functional, rather than unhealthy and dysfunctional. In particular, a great deal of recent research suggests that the more that people's reward systems are tuned to forming social connections with others, the more likely they are to be both more physically healthy and more psychologically well balanced. This is what makes internet pornography addiction so troubling. It represents a tuning of the reward system from a very healthy type of reward, that of forming a genuine and intimate connection with another, into a type of reward that removes the user from social contact, and often leaves them feeling lonely and ashamed rather than connected and supported.

It is a basic assumption of addiction research that when people describe themselves as experiencing the detrimental effects associated with pathological addictions, there is good reason to think that they really are addicted (in the more troubling clinical sense of the term). Few people will endure the humiliation of confessing to a pathological addiction which is not real. It is the reverse strategy, of denying an addiction that is obvious to loved ones, which is much more common. It is very clear, from the reports of the large number of individuals who suffer from it, that internet porn addiction is a real phenomenon. It is also clear that, in at least some cases, it takes a very severe and debilitating form.

The first-person accounts you will read in this book and collected on Gary's website of the same name will, and should, trouble you deeply. It is truly frightening to learn the degree to which internet pornography can damage and alienate individuals who have become badly addicted to watching it. At the same time, one of the most striking features of these reports is how they reflect a reversal of the damaging effects of internet porn addiction. It is truly beautiful to see people who have lost themselves in this addiction turn their lives around. Instead of compulsively masturbating in private, they have come to find meaning and genuine social connection through selfless attempts to help others caught in a similar trap. It all happens on the internet, both good and bad. Within this same technological medium, a medium which often threatens to make us impersonal, this group has found a way to move from an activity which is completely solitary and detached to something that is deeply altruistic, brave, personal and meaningful. It is time that the rest of us took note of what they are saying. Many physicians and researchers have dismissed and undermined these reports. However, that strategy is simply not ethical. We must respect the wisdom of their experience and the humility they show by sharing it. Anyone who pretends to care about the social and sexual health of others has a duty to better understand this phenomenon and find creative ways to reduce the damage it is doing.

Dr Anthony Jack
Professor of Philosophy, Psychology, Neurology and Neuroscience and Research Director at the Inamori International Center for Ethics and Excellence, Case Western Reserve University.

Introduction

I count him braver who overcomes his desires than him who conquers his enemies; for the hardest victory is over self.

Aristotle

You might be reading this book because you're curious why hundreds of thousands of porn users around the globe are experimenting with giving it up.[1] But more likely you're reading it because you are engaging with pornographic material in a way that you find troubling. Maybe you have been spending more time online seeking out graphic material than you want to, despite a settled determination to cut back. Maybe you are finding it difficult to climax during sex, or you're plagued by unreliable erections. Maybe you're noticing that real partners just don't excite you while the online sirens beckon constantly. Maybe you've escalated to fetish material that you find disturbing or out of alignment with your values or even your sexual orientation.

If you're anything like the thousands of other people who have realised that they have a problem, it has probably taken you a while to connect your troubles with your porn use. You might have thought you were struggling with some other disorder. Perhaps thought you had developed unaccustomed depression or social anxiety or, as one man feared, premature dementia. Or maybe you believed that you had low testosterone or were simply getting older. You might even have been prescribed drugs from a well-meaning doctor. Perhaps your physician assured you that you were wrong to worry about your use of pornography.

There are plenty of authoritative voices out there who will tell you that an interest in graphic imagery is perfectly normal, and that therefore internet porn is harmless. While the first claim is true, the second, as we shall see, is not. Although not all porn users develop problems, some do. At the moment, mainstream culture tends to assume that pornography use cannot cause severe symptoms. And, as high-profile criticisms of pornography often come from religious and socially conservative organizations, it's easy for liberally minded people to dismiss them without examination.

But for the last eight years, I have been paying attention to what people say about their experiences with pornography. For even longer, I've been studying what scientists are learning about how our brains work. I am here to tell you that this isn't about liberals and conservatives. It isn't about religious shame or sexual freedom.

This is about the nature of our brains and how they respond to cues from a radically changed environment. This is about the effects of chronic overconsumption of sexual novelty, delivered on demand in endless supply. This is about youthful access to limitless hardcore streaming videos – a phenomenon which is moving so quickly that researchers cannot stay current. For example, a 2008 study reported that 14.4 percent of boys were exposed to porn prior to age 13.[2] By the time stats were gathered in 2011, early exposure had jumped to 48.7 percent.[3] Similarly, daily porn viewing was rare in the 2008 study (5.2%), but by 2011, more than 13 percent of adolescents viewed porn daily or almost daily. What would these statistics be today given universal smartphone possession?

Until about half a dozen years ago I had no opinion about internet porn. I thought that two-dimensional images of women were a poor substitute for actual three-dimensional women. But I've never been in favour of banning porn. I grew up in a non-religious family in Seattle, the liberal Northwest. 'Live and let live' was my motto.

However, when men began showing up in my wife's website forum claiming to be addicted to porn it became clear that something serious was going on. A long-time anatomy and physiology teacher, I am particularly interested in neuroplasticity (how experiences alter the brain), the appetite mechanisms of the brain and, by extension, addiction. I'd been keeping up with the biological research in this area, intrigued by discoveries about the physiological underpinnings of our appetites and how they can become dysregulated.

The symptoms these men (and later women) described strongly suggested that their use of pornography had re-trained, and made significant material changes to, their brains. Psychiatrist Norman Doidge explains in his bestseller *The Brain That Changes Itself*:

> *The men at their computers looking at porn ... had been seduced into pornographic training sessions that met all the conditions required for plastic change of brain maps. Since neurons that fire together wire together, these men got massive amounts of practice wiring these images into the pleasure centres of the brain, with the rapt attention necessary for plastic change. ... Each time they felt sexual excitement and had an orgasm when they masturbated, a 'spritz of dopamine', the reward neurotransmitter, consolidated the connections made in the brain during the sessions. Not only did the reward facilitate the behaviour; it provoked none of the embarrassment they felt purchasing* Playboy *at a store. Here was a behaviour with no 'punishment', only reward.*
>
> *The content of what they found exciting changed as the Web sites introduced themes and scripts that altered their brains without their awareness. Because plasticity is competitive, the brain maps for new, exciting images increased at the expense of what had previously attracted them – the reason, I believe, they began to find their girlfriends less of a turn-on ...*
>
> *As for the patients who became involved in porn, most*

were able to go cold turkey once they understood the problem and how they were plastically reinforcing it. They found eventually that they were attracted once again to their mates.

The men on the forum found such material and the research underlying it both comforting and helpful. At last they understood how porn had hijacked the primitive appetite mechanisms of their brains. These ancient brain structures urge us toward evolutionarily beneficial behaviours including an appreciation of novel mates, helping to discourage inbreeding.

However, our behavioural choices in turn affect our neurochemical balance in these same brain structures. This is how chronic overconsumption can have unexpected effects. It can make us hyper-aroused by our favourite enticements, such that immediate wants weigh heavier than they should relative to longer term desires. It can also sour our enjoyment of – and responsiveness to – everyday pleasures. It can drive us to seek more extreme stimulation. Or cause withdrawal symptoms so severe that they send even the most strong-minded of us bolting for relief. It can also alter our mood, perception and priorities – all without our conscious awareness.

Armed with an account of 'how the machine works' that drew on the best available science, former porn users realized their brains were plastic and that there was a good chance they could reverse porn-induced changes. They decided it made no sense to wait for an expert consensus about whether internet porn was potentially harmful or not when they could eliminate it and track their own results.

These pioneers began to take control of their behaviour and steer for the results they wanted. They saw the gains from consistency without panicking about setbacks, which they accepted with greater self-compassion.

Along the way, they learned, and shared, some truly fascinating insights about recovery from internet porn-related problems – brand new discoveries that made the return to balance less harrowing for those following in their footsteps. That was fortunate because a flood of younger people, with far more malleable brains, were about to swell the ranks of those seeking relief from porn-related problems.

Sadly, many were motivated by severe sexual dysfunctions (delayed ejaculation, anorgasmia, erectile dysfunction and loss of attraction to real partners). Persistent porn-induced ED in young men caught the medical profession by surprise, but in 2014 doctors finally began to acknowledge it. Harvard urology professor and author of *Why Men Fake It: The Totally Unexpected Truth About Men and Sex,* Abraham Morgentaler said, 'it's hard to know exactly how many young men are suffering from porn-induced ED. But it's clear that this is a new phenomenon, and it's not rare.'[4] Another urologist and author Harry Fisch writes bluntly that porn is killing sex. In his book *The New Naked,* he zeroes in on the decisive element: the internet. It 'provided ultra-easy access to something that is fine as an occasional treat but hell for your [sexual] health on a daily basis.'[5]

In May, 2014, the prestigious medical journal *JAMA Psychiatry* published research showing that, even in moderate porn users, use (number of years and current hours per week) correlates with reduced grey matter and decreased sexual responsiveness. The study was subtitled "The Brain on Porn".[6] The researchers cautioned that the heavy porn users' brains might have been pre-shrunken rather than shrunken by porn usage, but favoured degree-of-porn-use as the most plausible explanation. Said lead author Simon Kühn:

> That could mean that regular consumption of pornography more or less wears out your reward system.

Then in July 2014, a team of neuroscience experts headed by a psychiatrist at Cambridge University revealed that more than half of the subjects in their study of porn addicts reported

> that as a result of excessive use of sexually explicit materials, they had ... experienced diminished libido or erectile function specifically in physical relationships with women (although not in relationship to the sexually explicit material).[7]

But the pioneers I'm describing didn't have the benefit of any formal confirmation. They worked it all out by exchanging self-reports.

I've written what follows to provide a straightforward summary of what we now know about the effects of pornography on some users, how it relates to the findings of neuroscience and evolutionary biology, and how best we can address the problems associated with pornography, both individually and collectively. If you're experiencing internet porn-related problems, give me a couple of hours of undivided attention, and there's a good chance that I can get you on the road to understanding your condition and dealing with it.

Now, how would a guy know if his sluggish sexual performance is related to his porn use or stems instead from performance anxiety (the standard diagnosis for guys without below-the-belt problems)?

1. First, see a good urologist and rule out any medical abnormality.

2. Next, on one occasion masturbate to your favourite porn (or simply imagine how it was if you've sworn off it).

3. Then, on another occasion masturbate with no porn and without fantasising about porn.

Compare the quality of your erections and the time it took to climax (if you *can* climax). A healthy young man should have no trouble attaining a full erection and masturbating to orgasm without porn or porn fantasy.

– If you have a strong erection in #2, but erectile dysfunction in #3, then you probably have porn-induced ED.

– If #3 is strong and solid, but you have trouble with a real partner, then you probably have anxiety-related ED.

– If you have problems during both #2 and #3, you may have progressive porn-induced ED or a below-the-belt problem for which you will need medical help.

I begin the book with an account of how internet porn addiction first became an issue as massive numbers of people with access to high-speed porn began talking about the problems they felt it had caused. I'll include first-hand accounts of how the phenomenon unfolded and the symptoms people commonly reported.

The subsequent chapter touches on contemporary neuroscience and the light it sheds on the delicate appetite mechanisms of the brain. I'll summarize some of the recent research on behavioural addiction, sexual conditioning and why adolescent brains are especially vulnerable in the face of a brain-training superstimulus like today's porn.

Chapter three recounts various commonsense approaches people have used to get clear of their porn-related problems as well as some pitfalls to avoid. I don't offer a set protocol. Everyone's circumstances are slightly different and there are no magic bullets. For example, tactics that work well for single people may have to be adapted by someone in a relationship. And younger guys who develop porn-induced ED sometimes need longer than older guys. Often several different approaches are helpful, concurrently or in sequence.

In the conclusion I'll consider why a consensus about porn's risks is still in the future, and which lines of research are most promising. Finally, I'll consider how society might help porn users to make more informed choices.

One final thing before we start. I am not saying that you *should* have a problem with porn. I am not trying to start some kind of moral panic, or to say what is and isn't 'natural' in human sexuality. If you don't feel you have a problem, then I am not about to argue with you. It's up to each of us to decide what we think about graphic sexual content and the industry that produces much of it.

But if you do feel that pornography is harming you, or someone you know, then read on, and I will do my best to explain how internet pornography can produce unexpected effects, and what you can do about it.

1

What Are We Dealing With?

It is not the answer that enlightens, but the question.
Eugene Ionesco

Most users regard internet porn as a solution – to boredom, sexual frustration, loneliness or stress. However, about seven years ago, some porn users started to connect various problems *with* their porn use. In 2012, a guy on an online forum known as Reddit/NoFap recounted the history of how men first figured out what they were dealing with. (The onomatopoeic term 'fap' is youthful slang for 'masturbation to porn'.):

> *Around 2008/2009, people started surfacing on the internet who were freaked out that they had erectile dysfunction, but at the same time they could get a solid erection to varying degrees of extreme porn with the help of some good old deathgrip [masturbation]. The weird thing was, that in some cases, thousands of people responded to these forum posts, saying they had the same exact symptoms.*
>
> *Now, taking those symptoms into account, people figured they'd desensitised themselves to real women by escalating to evermore extreme genres of porn and masturbating [such] that no woman's vagina could match the stimulation. They hoped/guessed that if they'd stop watching porn and masturbating for a significant amount of time this desentisation might be reversed.*
>
> *These people, who back then didn't have YBOP [www. yourbrainonporn.com], NoFap and dozens of other forums*

on the subject, thought they were alone. The only weird-ass freaks on the planet who can't get it up to a real woman, but find disgusting genres of porn a turn on. A lot of them were still virgins. Others were failing for years with real women, which devastated their confidence. They figured that they would never be able to have a normal fulfilling relationship with a woman, and considering they were freaks of nature, they secluded themselves from society and became hermits. ...

[Quitting porn] helped reverse the porn-induced ED of these guys, and besides normal libido they started reporting other positive changes too: depression and social anxiety going away, increased confidence, the feeling of fulfilment and being on top of the world...

I'm one of those guys. I'd had several failures with women, starting in the middle of puberty. This had become the single most devastating thing to my psyche. In this modern world, where there's hardly a commercial, a movie, a TV show, or a conversation without sexual innuendos, I was constantly reminded of my weirdness. I was a failure as a man on a very fundamental level and I seemed to be the only one.

A year before I [quit porn] I'd even gone to see psychiatrists and psychologists, who diagnosed me with severe social anxiety disorder and depression, and wanted to put me on antidepressants, which I never agreed to.

When I found out that the central problem of my life that was on my mind 24/7 could be reversed, the heaviest rock was lifted from my heart. When I went on my first NoFap streak (cca 80 days) I started noticing similar superpowers as reported by others. Is that really so weird? The central thing destroying my confidence and making me feel alone on the planet of 7 billion was being reversed, and it turned out to be very common.

Today, on my 109th day of a streak, I feel happy, confident, social, smart, capable of meeting any challenge, etc., etc.

The earliest people to report porn-related problems in online forums were typically computer programmers and information-technology specialists. They had acquired high-speed internet porn ahead of the pack – and then developed uncharacteristic sexual tastes, delayed ejaculation or erectile dysfunction (ED) during sex. Eventually, some experienced ED even while using porn. Nearly all were in their late twenties or older.

As one such forum member noted, internet porn was *different,* oddly irresistible:

> *With the magazines, porn use was a few times a week and I could basically regulate it 'cause it wasn't really that 'special'. But when I entered the murky world of internet porn, my brain had found something it just wanted more and more of. I was out of control in less than 6 months. Years of mags: no problems. A few months of online porn: hooked.*

A bit of history gives us some clues as to why today's pornography might have unexpected effects on the brain. Visual pornography entered the mainstream with magazines, but users had to content themselves with static erotica. Each instalment's novelty and its arousal potential faded fairly quickly, and a person either had to go back to fantasizing about his hot neighbour, or make a substantial, perhaps awkward or costly, foray to obtain more material. There were a few x-rated movies and some of them were big commercial successes. Dedicated fans of hardcore could also find sexually explicit clips in adult bookstores. But supply was still restricted to a handful of public or semi-public venues and most people didn't want to spend much time in movie houses or peepshow booths.

Then came video rentals and late-night cable channels. These media were more stimulating than static porn[8] and much less awkward to access than a film at the cinema. Yet how many times could a person watch the same video before it was time for another trip to the video shop (and a break)? Viewers often had to watch a story line with an erotic build-up before getting to the hot stuff. Most minors still had very limited access.

Next, porn viewers turned to dial-up: private, cheaper, but mostly stills ... at first. People could access it more easily, but it was slow. Material could not be consumed at a click:

> *You had to download the video, then open it and risk getting a virus. Sometimes you didn't have the right software, so you spent a lot of time making sure it was what you wanted to see before downloading it and 'enjoying' it, or you would go to a specific site whose content you liked, watch the one or two new videos and leave it at that.*

All that was about to change.

In 2006, high-speed internet gave rise to a whole new creature: galleries of short porn clips of the hottest few minutes of an unending supply of streaming hardcore videos. They are called 'tube sites' because they stream like YouTube videos. The world of porn has never been the same. Users describe the transformation:

> *I'd looked at pictures for years (well over a decade), and video clips from time to time. But when the tube sites became my daily fare, it was only shortly afterward that I developed ED problems. I think the tube sites, with their endless clips immediately accessible, threw my brain into overload.*

*

> *On a tube site you go straight from 0 to 140 kph. Arousal isn't a slow, relaxed, teasing build-up of expectation. It is*

straight to full-on orgasmic action. Because tube clips are so short, you do a LOT more clicking to novel clips for various reasons: One is way too short to build up arousal; you don't know what will be in the clip till you watch it; endless curiosity, etc.

*

I can totally relate to 'wanting to watch 10 videos all at once, streaming at the same time...' It's amazing to hear someone else say it. It's like this sensory overload, or hoarding, or just overstuffing yourself with your favourite junk food.

*

Tube sites, especially the big ones, are the crack cocaine of internet pornography. There is so much of it, and so much new content every day, every hour, every 10 minutes that I was always able to find constant new stimulation.

*

Now with high-speed, even to smartphones, it has made me continuously watch more and more and at higher resolution. It sometimes becomes a whole day affair looking for the perfect one to finish on. It never, ever satisfies. 'Need more' the brain always says...such a lie.

*

Before I discovered I had ED I had escalated to tube-site compilation videos, each consisting of the hottest few seconds of dozens of hardcore videos.

*

Highspeed porn changed everything. I began masturbating more than once a day. If I didn't feel like masturbating, but wanted to relieve stress or go to sleep, porn helped me get aroused. I found myself looking at porn prior to sex with my wife because she just couldn't do it for me anymore. Delayed ejaculation was a huge problem: I could no longer orgasm from oral sex and I sometimes had difficulty with orgasm in a vagina.

Deep in a primitive part of the brain, surfing tube sites registers as really valuable because of all the sexual novelty. The extra excitement strengthens brain circuits that urge you to use porn again. Your own sexual fantasies pale in comparison. According to one German research team[9], users' problems correlated most closely with the number of screens opened (variety) and degree of arousal, not with time spent viewing online porn.

Another risk of today's online porn buffet is overconsumption. University of Massachusetts Medical School professor Sherry Pagoto PhD[10] writes:

Studies on appetite show that variety is strongly associated with overconsumption. You will eat more at a buffet than you will when meatloaf is the only thing on the table. In neither scenario will you leave hungry but in one you will leave regretful. In other words, [if you want to circumvent overconsumption and its problems] avoid the buffets of life.

It's also worth noting that videos replace imagination in a way that still images don't. Left strictly to our imaginations we humans once tended to assume the starring role in our sexual fantasies, not the passive role of mere voyeur as in video-watching. However, some of those who start regular porn use very young are having a different experience:

'Alien' is the word I'd use to describe how it felt when I tried to have sex with real women. It felt artificial and foreign to me. It's like I've gotten so conditioned to sitting in front of a

screen jerking it, that my mind considers that to be normal
sex instead of real actual sex.

During real sex viewers aren't in the position of a voyeur, let
alone a voyeur of a particular body part or very specific fetish
that many of them have been viewing for years before they
connect with a partner.

An Elephant in the Room

At the end of 2010, my wife suggested I set up an online resource
about this new phenomenon. By then, her forum on sexual
relationships had been overrun by men seeking clues about
their porn-related problems: loss of attraction to real partners,
delayed ejaculation or complete inability to orgasm during
sex, alarming new sexual tastes as they escalated through
porn fetishes, even unaccustomed premature ejaculation. She
felt they needed a dedicated website where they could read
each others' self reports and keep up on the new research on
internet addiction, sexual conditioning and neuroplasticity.
From this came the website Your Brain On Porn (YBOP).

Curious as to who was linking to the new resource I began
tracking my visitors. I was astonished. Links to the new site
popped up in threads all over the web, often in other languages.
Men worldwide were looking for answers. At present, YBOP
gets as many as 20,000 unique visitors a day. Forums for people
quitting porn are popping up and growing rapidly. The largest
and oldest English-language forum is Reddit/NoFap (2011)
with some 132,000 members at present. Reddit/PornFree
boasts 19,000, NoFap.org 30,000, RebootNation.org 2,500,
and YourBrainRebalanced 13,000. The same phenomenon is
occurring internationally. For example, in China, two forums
combined currently have more than a million members
struggling to recover from internet porn's effects.[11]

Wherever men congregated one could find them debating

porn's effects. Threads – sometimes thousands of posts long – appeared on websites for body-builders, 'pick-up artists', university alumni, those seeking medical advice, car enthusiasts, sports fans, recreational drug users, even guitarists!

Most guys could not believe porn was the culprit behind their symptoms until months after they quit:

> *After years of porn, I was having trouble with erections. It had been getting worse and worse for a couple years. Needed more and more types of porn stimulation. I was really worried, but the anxiety just pushed me deeper into more extreme porn. Now, the more I go without porn, masturbation, fantasy and orgasm, the more difficult it becomes to not get an erection. LOL. No ED problems or weak ejaculations like I had just a few months ago. I have healed.*

Even after quitting and seeing improvements, many were still sceptical. They returned to internet porn – only to see their problems gradually (or swiftly) recur. And even though anonymous online forums were buzzing, no one wanted to talk about it publicly:

> *Young guys won't go to doctors talking about ED. Porn-induced ED and porn addiction are our personal secret. We're too anxious, ashamed, confused and angry to create awareness of these issues. We hide in the shadows because we individually don't want to be seen to exist. Therefore we collectively aren't thought to exist.*

For some, quitting triggered distressing, unexpected withdrawal symptoms:

> *Here's what I'm dealing with: irritability, fatigue, inability to sleep (even sleep aids don't help much), trembling/shaking, lack of focus, shortness of breath, and depression.*

*

I've battled a few addictions in my life, from nicotine to alcohol and other substances. I've overcome all of them, and this was by far the most difficult. Urges, crazy thoughts, sleeplessness, feelings of hopelessness, despair, worthlessness, and many more negative things were all part of what I went through with this porn thing. It's a wicked awful thing that I will never have to deal with ever again in my life – ever.

If you don't realise such symptoms are connected with quitting, but you *do* notice that returning to porn relieves them, then you are strongly motivated to keep using porn. I'll come back to the withdrawal-symptom hurdle in the recovery chapter.

Most alarmingly of all, those with erectile dysfunction who quit porn often reported temporary, but absolute, loss of libido and abnormally lifeless genitals. Even men with no ED sometimes experienced temporary loss of libido and mild sexual dysfunctions soon after they quit:

I have absolutely no sex drive. No spontaneous erections. It's a very strange feeling when you look at a beautiful woman and in your head you have your normal thoughts like 'Wow, she's beautiful. I would like to get to know her!' and yet you have no sexual thoughts or intentions. It's a very strange and for me quite a scary experience. It's like you've been castrated.

Unless guys had been warned about this 'flatline', fears of permanent impotence sent them rushing back to cyberspace to attempt to salvage their manhood. Escalating to more extreme porn, even with a partially flaccid penis, seemed a small price to pay to stem the total loss of libido. Porn use seemed like a cure.

Many, however, were horrified to discover that they *couldn't* override the flatline by returning to porn. They had to wait until their libido returned naturally – which sometimes took months.

Interestingly, male rats who copulate to sexual exhaustion also show evidence of a mini-flatline[12] before their libido returns. Is the porn-induced flatline biologically related? Researchers study rats because their primitive brain structures are surprisingly similar to ours. As developmental molecular biologist John J. Medina PhD says, animal research 'acts as a guiding "flashlight" for human research, illuminating biological processes'.[12] In other words, researchers aren't studying rats to help *them* with their addictions, erections and mood disorders.

Happily, once warned about the possibility of a temporary flatline, most guys powered through it with relative equanimity:

> *About my flatline. When people say they feel like their cock is dead, they aren't exaggerating. It literally feels lifeless. It feels like a burden to have to carry it around.*

As tube sites became more popular and more widely accessed, a flood of younger guys in their early twenties and late teens arrived with the *same* sexual dysfunctions as the older visitors. Rapidly, they comprised the majority of visitors to the websites where men were complaining of what they understood to be porn-induced sexual dysfunctions.

The Other Porn Experiment

In 2012, guys in their early twenties began to set up online forums dedicated entirely to experimenting with giving up internet porn in hopes of reversing porn-related problems. Often they found that it helped to cut out masturbation temporarily too. Indeed, many were unable to masturbate without porn, at least early in the process. Their goal was to give their brains a rest from chronic overstimulation via internet erotica. They called their approach 'rebooting.'

The best-known English-language forum is Reddit/NoFap. Other popular English-language forums include Reboot Nation, Reddit/PornFree, YourBrainRebalanced and NoFap. org.[13] Women are welcome at all of them and their numbers are growing too. I've been monitoring some of these forums since their inception because members frequently link to YBOP.

As part of this grassroots movement, largely beneath the radar of the mainstream press, thousands of people worldwide have undertaken the groundbreaking experiment of giving up artificial online sexual stimulation (internet porn, web-cam encounters, erotic literature, surfing escort ads, etc.,). Many have shared their results over a period of months.

This vast experiment has been conducted without controls or double-blind protocols (such trials would be impossible because researchers would have to ask some participants to stop masturbating to porn, which is the sort of thing people – whether they're researchers or subjects – notice). It is the only experiment I know of that removes the variable of porn use and compares histories with subsequent outcomes.

Obviously, 'subjects' are not randomly chosen. They are people who want to experiment with giving up porn. Also, the vast majority are digital natives, not a cross-section of the general population. Moreover, although membership on these porn-challenge forums has mushroomed since the first one started in 2011, they don't reveal the precise percentages of people with porn-related problems in any age group.

Sceptics sometimes claim that people who experiment with quitting must be motivated by religious reasons. Yet all of the forums named above are secular. The largest of these new forums, and likely youngest in terms of average age, conducted a self-poll a couple of years ago. Only 7% had joined for religious reasons.[15]

The information these online forums and threads generate is anecdotal, but it would be a mistake to dismiss it without further investigation. For one thing, the people quitting porn and seeing benefits are surprisingly diverse. They come from different backgrounds, cultures and degrees of religiosity; some are on psychotropic medications; some are in relationships; some smoke and use recreational drugs; some are bodybuilders; their ages cover a wide range, and so forth.

For another thing, in this informal experiment the subjects generally remove the variable of internet porn use. With the exception of one 3-week, formal experiment, "A Love That Doesn't Last: Pornography consumption and weakened commitment to one's romantic partner",[16] no academic studies have ever removed the variable of porn use. Other porn studies are correlational. They can tell us interesting things about what conditions are *associated* with porn use, but they can't show us what shifts when users remove porn. The latter is one way scientists verify a causal connection.

Existing studies do find that frequency of porn viewing correlates with depression, anxiety, stress and social (mal) functioning,[17] as well as less sexual and relationship satisfaction and altered sexual tastes,[18] poorer quality of life and health,[19] and real-life intimacy problems.[20] But so far, researchers seldom, if ever, ask about other phenomena seen regularly on the forums, such as impaired motivation and confidence, brain fog (inability to focus), loss of attraction to real people, sexual dysfunction, escalation to what users themselves describe as more extreme material over time, and so forth.

In any case, people who have been using porn heavily since puberty rarely make the connection between their porn use and symptoms such as anxiety, depression or weak erections until after they stop using. No matter how miserable they are, porn seems like a way to feel good – a solution rather than a source of problems.

Meanwhile, there's little point in a researcher asking such people if their porn use has caused their symptoms. Porn users have not been given any reason to consider that possibility. Society has already put their problems in neat little boxes that do not take account of internet porn use. Today's porn users are regularly diagnosed with – and prescribed medication for – social anxiety, low self-esteem, concentration problems, lack of motivation, depression, performance anxiety (even when they also can't achieve an erection or climax on their own – unless they use porn), and so forth.

Some quietly suffer with panic that their sexual orientations have mysteriously morphed, or that they must be closet perverts because they eventually can *only* get off to fetish porn, or that they will never be able to have sex, and thus intimacy, because of their sexual dysfunctions. Not to be alarmist, but I read far too many recovery accounts that mention earlier suicidal thoughts. Disturbingly, recent research at Oxford University found that moderate or severe addiction to the internet was associated with increased risk for self-harm.[21] Here are comments by three guys:

I have seriously considered suicide throughout my life because of these issues but I was able to cope until I found out porn was the problem. 115 days later I have finally broken free of its chains. It's still tough, but I know if I don't use it I'll be able to have sex with my beautiful girlfriend the next day.

*

Staying off porn really makes a difference! I thought it was impossible to quit porn to the point of contemplating castration and suicide. Here's one thing I actually didn't know that helped me out: People who view 'transsexual' porn do it because of all the stimulation, and even the producers admit that they make this fetish for a straight audience. My thoughts that I might have been bi/gay were more of an optical/psychological illusion.

*

As a child I was highly athletic, smart, and sociable. I was always happy and had a million friends. That all changed around age 11 when I downloaded KaZaA and progressed to nearly every type of porn imaginable (dominatrix, animal, amputee, etc.). I started having severe depression and anxiety. The next 15 years of my life were completely miserable. I was incredibly anti-social. I didn't talk to anybody and sat alone at lunch. I hated everyone. I quit all the sports that I played even though I was top rank in all of them. My marks plummeted to barely passable. As much as I hate to think about it now, I had even started thinking about planning my own 'Columbine style' exit to this world.

After people quit using porn, the benefits they report are often staggering. Indirectly, their experience suggests that some brains have been profoundly affected by today's superstimulating high-speed porn. As we'll see, formal research is now starting to bear out their reports.

Given the weight of first person testimony from these forums worldwide, the emphasis should be on further research that sheds light on the mechanics of what is actually happening. Research could also help sort the porn-afflicted from those with other disorders, such as those stemming from childhood trauma and attachment problems. It goes without saying that not everyone's problems can be traced back to internet porn use. It also goes without saying that an attraction to transgender people, an interest in being dominated, and any number of other things, can form part of a durable and happy sexual identity. The problem is in the effects of porn on the brain, not in any particular aspect of human beings' astonishing diversity in matters of desire.

Common Symptoms

Although most early trials in giving up internet porn were desperate ploys to reverse deteriorating sexual function, today many people make the experiment in order to gain a whole range of benefits. In this section you'll find a sprinkling of self-reports describing improvements after quitting porn, broken down into categories. But many users see a wide range of diverse improvements. For example, this ex-user wrote:

Improvements since quitting:

– Social anxiety improved drastically – includes confidence, eye contact, comfort interacting, smoothness, etc.

– More energy in general

– Clearer, sharper mind, more concentration

– More vibrant looking face

– Depression alleviated

– Desire to interact with women

– Boners are back!!

Another guy described himself *during* his porn use:

– My friends were drifting away. I gave up socialising to sit in my room and pleasure myself.

– My family loved me unconditionally, but did not enjoy my company.

– I had trouble focusing on my job and as well as my classes at my university.

– I had no girlfriend.

– I had an enormous amount of anxiety with human interactions in general.

– I worked out furiously, but never seemed to gain anything.

– Everyone told me I was mentally checked out. I even caught a glimpse of me in a video and you could see a blank stare in my eyes. No one was home. Definition of space cadet.

– No ENERGY, no matter how much I slept, NONE. NOTHING. AT ALL. Always tired. Bags under my eyes, pale, acne, and dehydrated.

– I was terribly depressed.

– I had porn-induced ED.

– I was stressed, anxious, confused, and lost.

– I was not living life, but I was not dead either. I was a zombie.

People naturally wonder how such disparate symptoms could be associated with internet porn use, and what physiological changes might be behind the improvements. They also wonder why some users see different results or no results. Solid research on internet porn's effects is just beginning, but in the next chapter I'll hypothesize based on the abundant relevant science already available on brain plasticity and internet use.

Meanwhile, let's take a closer look at people's accounts of what they're experiencing.

Interfering with life, losing control

Inability to control use and use that interferes with one's life are two cardinal signs of addiction. Priorities have shifted due to changes in the brain that we'll look at later. In effect, life's natural rewards, such as friendship, exercise and accomplishment, can no longer compete. Your brain now believes that IT – in this case internet porn use – is an important goal, and equates it with your survival:

Most days I would wank so much that by the end of the day when I orgasmed nothing would even come out. ED my first time sent me into a porn spiral. I would literally wake up, roll over and masturbate, masturbate all day, then at night masturbate and go to sleep. 6 times a day or more, no joke. Safe to say my life was an absolute mess, all the bad effects of porn x 10. I knew that the porn and masturbation was affecting me but I was in denial, masturbation is good for you right? You can't be addicted to porn.

*

My lowest point was when I lost out on my pharmacy diploma and lost my girlfriend on the same day, due to porn and procrastination.

*

I used transgender porn to get hard so I could finish with heterosexual porn. Without realizing, I was soon watching a lot of taboo and extreme porn that I never would have considered a couple of years ago. I couldn't believe I let myself get to this point. I just couldn't stop myself.

*

(Female) I can get off a ridiculous amount of times in one night because the female biological makeup allows it. Many females (not all) spend a lot of time not with porn, but with erotica. We fantasise a lot to get off, while men are very visual. With the internet, it's easy to find erotica everywhere, and there are entire forums dedicated to the type of erotica you want. At my worst, I would have 7 or 8 different sites open and go through them for about 3 or 4 hours or more looking for the perfect sex story to get off on.

*

I thought that it was due to an increased libido that I watched so much porn. Now I know I was wrong. I had an addiction. I barely went out and most certainly didn't have any female contacts.

*

Before I quit I felt like shit 24/7. I had zero energy, and zero motivation. I was lethargic for every hour of every day. I didn't eat right. I didn't exercise. I didn't study. I didn't care about personal hygiene. And I could not care. In the state that I was in, it was extremely difficult to stand for more than 3 minutes, let alone do something productive. I'm over a month now and I feel so much better.

*

Everything from my social life to my physical health has been damaged by this addiction. The worst part about it was that I constantly justified it in my head by saying it was 'healthy for me' and 'at least it isn't a drug'. In reality, this was worse than any drug I have consumed and the least healthy activity I was participating in.

*

During the heights of my porn addiction, I never looked forward to much of anything: dreaded going to work, and never saw socializing with friends and family as all that great, especially in comparison to my porn rituals, which gave me more pleasure and stimulation than anything else. With the addiction gone, little things make me really happy. I find myself laughing often, smiling for no real reason, and just being in good spirits all around.

*

I thought I was a pessimist, but really I was just an addict.

Inability to orgasm during sex

Years of porn use can cause a variety of symptoms, which when examined, lie on a spectrum. Often porn users report that delayed ejaculation (DE) or inability to orgasm (anorgasmia) was a precursor to full blown erectile dysfunction. Any of the following may precede or accompany delayed ejaculation and erectile dysfunction:

– Earlier genres of porn are no longer exciting.

– Uncharacteristic fetishes develop.

– Porn use is more sexually exciting than a partner.

– Sensitivity of penis decreases.

– Sexual arousal with sexual partners declines.

– Erections fade when attempting penetration or shortly thereafter.

– Penetrative sex is not stimulating.

– Porn fantasy is necessary to maintain erection or interest with partner.

A few examples:

I'm so happy right now! I'm a 25-year old male and until last night I had never orgasmed in the presence of a female. I have had sex but never, ever been close to climaxing through any stimulation whatsoever. I started out like most of you, using internet porn from around the age of 15. If only I'd known what I was doing to myself.

*

(Age 29) 17 years of masturbation and 12 years of escalating

to extreme/fetish porn. I started to lose interest in real sex. The build up and release from porn became stronger than it was from sex. Porn offers unlimited variety. I could choose what I want to see in the moment. My delayed ejaculation during sex became so bad that sometimes I couldn't orgasm at all. This killed my last desire to have sex.

*

I've lived with delayed ejaculation all my life and I've never found anyone (including docs) who are familiar with the dysfunction or have any suggestions for improving it. I began using Viagra and Cialis to help me keep it up long enough to have an orgasm – often well over an hour of intense stimulation. I thought regular doses of porn were also necessary. Good news: by staying away from porn, I am now experiencing some of the most satisfying sex of my life with no ED meds; and I've got two decades on most of you. My erections are more frequent, firmer and longer lasting, and our lovemaking is relaxing and lasts as long as both of us want it to.

*

(4 months without porn) Yesterday was my birthday, and my girlfriend and I had sex. We've been sexually active for months, but I had never orgasmed once during sex, until yesterday. It was the greatest feeling ever. It's a huge weight lifted off both my shoulders and my girlfriend's, as she was feeling rather self-conscious about the issue.

*

I had some pretty bad delayed ejaculation problems with my previous girlfriend. I'm talking 2-3 hours of sex for me to be able to get off (so usually I ended up just stopping and going home and fapping).

*

My success continues in week 10 of my reboot...an even

better session with the missus tonight. Not only did I blow my load relatively quickly (defeating DE), I did it without having to go as vigorously as I usually would to finish. I went slow all the way, like never before, and it was brilliant. I could even say that I tried to back right off towards the end as I didn't want to finish so soon! Not bad for someone with a bad case of DE for a number of years.

Unreliable erections during sexual encounters

As mentioned, on most forums ED is the number-one reason men choose to give up porn. Eminent urologist Harry Fisch, MD is also seeing porn-related sexual dysfunctions in his practice. In *The New Naked* he writes:

I can tell how much porn a man watches as soon as he starts talking candidly about any sexual dysfunction he has. ... A man who masturbates frequently can soon develop erection problems when he's with his partner. Add porn to the mix, and he can become unable to have sex. ... A penis that has grown accustomed to a particular kind of sensation leading to rapid ejaculation will not work the same way when it's aroused differently. Orgasm is delayed or doesn't happen at all.

Urologist Carlo Foresta, President of the Italian Society of Reproductive Pathophysiology and author of some 300 academic studies, has been tracking the effects of internet porn for close to a decade. In a 2014 lecture, he highlighted the results of his annual surveys of high school seniors from 2005 to 2013. He saw a doubling of teens experiencing sexual problems. The most dramatic was a 600% jump in 'low sexual desire' in just eight years (from 1.7% to 10.3%).[22] Says Foresta, 'When the frequency of access to pornographic sites become routine...[it] results in a reduction or loss of sexual desire.'[23]

Next, Foresta compared regular porn users with non-regular users (ages 19-25). The former reported more erectile difficulties and half the sexual desire levels of their peers.[24]

A 2014 study on the US military (ages 21-40) found that ED rates had doubled between 2004 and 2013.[25] Apparently US civilians are experiencing problems too. In a 2014 poll of young voters (ages 18-40), 33 percent said porn was having a negative effect on their sex lives. Another nineteen percent were unsure.[26]

Also in 2014 a Canadian sexologists' study[27] showed that problems in sexual functioning are curiously higher in adolescent males than in adult males (which are already rising). Said researchers:

> *53.5% [of male teens] were classified as reporting symptoms indicative of a sexual problem. Erectile dysfunction and low desire were the most common.*

High rates of limp penises and low sexual desire in teenage males should make everyone take notice as being extremely surprising. Imagine how unheard of these conditions would be in young bulls and stallions. Yet the sexologists conducting the research were 'unclear' why they found such high rates, and didn't even mention internet porn overuse as a possible influence. The recent Cambridge study by addiction neuroscientists stated that almost 60% of the addicts they examined, 'experienced diminished libido or erectile function specifically in physical relationships with women (although not in relationship to the sexually explicit material)' as a result of excessive porn use.[28]

I have seen two diverging patterns of recovery. A few men bounce back in a relatively short time: about 2-3 weeks. Perhaps their difficulties are due to mild conditioning, excessive levels of masturbation (fuelled by internet porn), or a minor case of desensitisation (an addiction-related change we'll discuss in the next chapter).

The vast majority of guys need 2-6 months (or longer) to *fully* recover. Most 'long-rebooters' experience a variety of withdrawal symptoms, including the dreaded flatline. Typically, they are younger guys who started early on internet porn. I suspect that this unfortunate trend is the natural outcome of highly malleable adolescent brains[29] colliding with internet porn:

When I lost my virginity it really did not feel that good. I was bored actually. I lost the erection after maybe ten minutes. She wanted more sex, but I was done. The next time I tried to have sex with a woman was a disaster. I had an erection at first, but I lost it before I ever penetrated. Condom use was out of the question – not a hard enough erection.

*

My lowest point was when I couldn't get it up for my girlfriend (now ex-girlfriend) not once, but repeatedly over the course of our three-year relationship. We also never orgasmed from vaginal intercourse. I was visiting doctors; buying books on penis exercises; trying to change habits by masturbating to POV porn (instead of the extreme porn I was addicted to). She was totally supportive of me the entire time (this girl really loved me with all her heart). She even bought nice lingerie and made efforts to be the 'slut in the bedroom'. BUT even with that, I wasn't turned on because the porn I was into was much more extreme than that (rape, forced sex).

*

I never had a problem getting hard for porn, but when it came to the real thing, I started taking Cialis. Over time, I took more, and even then there were times when it would only partly work. WTH? Yet I could still get hard to porn.

In contrast, most older guys began their solo-sex careers with a catalogue, a magazine, a video, grainy TV porn, or amazingly (to today's young guys), their imagination. They also generally had *some* sex, or at least courtship, with a real partner before they fell under the spell of high-speed porn. Their 'real sex' brain pathways may temporarily be overwhelmed by hyperstimulating internet porn, but those pathways are still operational once the distraction of porn is removed:

> *(Married, 52) I have many decades of porn under my belt (so to speak). I have not looked at any porn or masturbated for nearly 4 weeks, and all I can say is the change is dramatic. This morning, I woke up with one of the most intense erections I have ever had. My wife noticed, and was nice enough to give me a wonderful BJ, all before 7 AM! Prior to this, I cannot remember ever waking up like this, except when I was a teen. Plus, the feeling was very intense, much better than any porn release I remember.*

*

> *(Married, age 50) I never thought I had ED. I managed to have sex with my wife. Boy, was I wrong! Since my recovery, my erections are way bigger, fuller and longer and the head is flared. My wife comments each time. I also remain erect even after orgasm, and think I could keep it up for a loooong time. My morning wood is also bigger and fuller. I really had ED and was too caught in my addiction to realize it. Keep in mind I am 50, though in pretty good shape for my age and clean living.*

*

> *The reward for 4 months of no porn has been an improved sex life with my wife, and after nearly fifteen years of being together, that is a considerable reward. Hurrah for plain 'vanilla' sex. I seem to feel more than I used to.*

Here's a guy in the middle, who started out on internet porn, but not high-speed:

> *I masturbated a lot from 13 and used porn from 14. Gradually, it took more to turn me on: bigger fantasies or harder porn, and I stopped getting hard without touching. During sex I would struggle to get an erection or keep it, especially for intercourse. Over the past 7 years I haven't held down a relationship, and the main reason for me has been this problem. Now, the good news: When I realized the cause, I immediately gave up porn. Over the last 6 weeks I held off masturbating as much as I possibly could. (My best record was 9 days!) It all paid off. I just went away with a girl for the weekend and it was the best ever. I still get pretty anxious from all the bad experiences over the years. But I just wanted to tell you all it can work, and it's well worth it!*

What about women? Porn use also seems to affect the sexual responsiveness of some women:

> *For us girls a moderate porn-related 'ED' is tough to spot, but I feel it the same way as guys describe it. There is desire but no arousal. No throbbing, pulling, overwhelming, pleasurable sensation in the clitoris and the lower abdomen, only a kind of mental push towards climax. And I **too** have PE [premature ejaculation], except it might more accurately be described as PO [premature orgasm]: orgasming while excitation is low, with the quality of the orgasm quite mediocre and unannounced except for a kind of anxiety-like tension localized in the genitals.*

Unaccustomed premature ejaculation

Although rare when compared to ED or delayed ejaculation, heavy porn users do sometimes report this symptom. Premature ejaculation from porn use may seem counterintuitive. Two possible explanations come to mind. Perhaps a guy has trained his nervous system to ejaculate very quickly (or while partially erect). As this man described:

Masturbation/porn can cause PE especially when you start doing it young. You want to reach climax/orgasm quickly because of the fear of being caught. So you teach your mind that when you're hard your job is to cum quickly and not enjoy the interim sensation.

For others porn may become a powerful trigger due to a strong association between porn and ejaculation. This automatic, high arousal response is similar to Pavlov's dog salivating at the sound of a bell:

I am no longer experiencing the extreme PE that I had for many years prior to reboot. It is really a miracle, because I had always just assumed it was some genetic defect. I did not connect the dots as possibly being porn-induced. Prior to my re-boot, my erect penis was very sensitive (hyper-sensitive) making ejaculation embarrassingly easy (quick). My penis would get rock hard and stand at attention at 12 o'clock, the skin stretched tight like a snare drum. My penis was a fuelled rocket sitting on the launch pad. Countdown starts at 10 seconds, 9, 8, 7, 6,5,4,3,2 … 1, ORGASM. The words 'Sorry dear' became my motto. But today, 52 days into re-boot, my penis is no longer on the rocket launch pad. It stands at 10 o'clock. I have a softer, but bigger erection. Don't get me wrong. It is still very hard and capable of vaginal penetration, just more plastic, less rigid, less sensitive, and not as explosive. Most important to my relationship with my wife, I am able to last longer. The reboot is working very well on my porn-induced PE!

*

When you watch porn you become over-stimulated and ejaculation is one stroke away. I've spoken to numerous men older than me and have asked them how they last long. Many said that they last long naturally and don't watch porn or masturbate. My cousin who says he lasts 20-30 minutes has said he lasts longer when he doesn't watch porn or masturbate.

*

I was going out with my now ex-girlfriend for 2 years before we broke up. I never had any sexual problem (be it ED or PE). I wasn't addicted to porn, although I masturbated to it occasionally. After we broke up, I used porn regularly and started going to massage parlours with happy endings. After 6 months, I got back with the same girl, and I somewhat reduced the frequency of my other activities. The sex was awful with my girlfriend (or at least it was for her). I didn't have a problem with getting it up (except maybe a couple of times), but I couldn't last for over a minute. The relationship endured a year, during which, I didn't, not even once, make her orgasm from penetration. The same girl I was giving multiple orgasms 6 months earlier.

For others, PE may be related to a history of forcing orgasms with weak erections:

I would force myself to ejaculate in the morning before school, and several times after. I wasn't even horny or hard, merely compelled by some urge to keep forcing myself to cum. My mechanistic porn habits have taken away all sensuality from the act of orgasm, turning it into a short spurt and muscle memory twitch of a climax. If you have porn-induced PE consider the new behaviours, feelings and sensations that came with its onset. Before, orgasms were absolutely phenomenal (my f--king knees would literally shake), but now I cum with a mechanical twitch and no sort of real gratitude toward the act (and that is including with women). If feels different and lame.

Alarming porn fetish tastes

Once upon a time, men could trust their penises to tell them everything they needed to know about their sexual tastes or orientation. That was before readily available porn videos.

Brains are plastic. The truth is we are always training our brains – with or without our conscious participation. It's clear from countless reports that it's not uncommon for porn users to move from genre to genre, often arriving at places they find personally disturbing and confusing. What might be behind this phenomenon?

One possibility is boredom or habituation meeting the developing adolescent brain. Teens are thrill seeking and easily bored. They love novelty. The stranger the better. Many a young man has described masturbating with one hand while clicking through videos with the other hand. Lesbian porn grows boring, so he tries out transgender porn. Novelty and anxiety ensue – and both increase sexual arousal. Before he knows it he has climaxed and a new association begins imprinting his sexual circuits.

Never before have developing adolescents been able to switch from genre to genre while masturbating. This casual practice may turn out to be a prime danger of today's porn:

I wasn't interested in any weird stuff before I started to watch internet porn. Just real girls of my age. Now, I like BBB, BBW, MILF, Tranny, Crossdresser, Fat, Skinny, and Teen. Once, I saw few seconds of a bisexual video (one woman, two guys) and I started to feel that 'taboo' feeling, but I didn't give it a chance, did not masturbate to it, and changed the video. So, I don't watch bisexual videos and

*have no cravings for them. That's because I didn't give them
a chance. But I gave a chance to every kind of porn I got into.
If I had given granny porn a chance, I would like it now too.*

The tendency to escalate to more extreme porn is not confined
to teens. In a pre-internet study, subjects were exposed either to
common, nonviolent porn or to innocuous videos for one hour
in each of six consecutive weeks. Two weeks later they were
provided with an opportunity to watch videotapes in privacy,
with a choice of G-rated, R-rated, and X-rated videos. The
subjects who had watched pornography showed little interest
in viewing nonviolent porn, electing instead to view bondage,
sadomasochism and bestiality. This consumption preference
was much more pronounced in males, though present to some
extent in females.[30]

In a review of relevant research, one of the study's authors
commented that consumers of pornography are not likely to
limit themselves to common porn when given the opportunity
to consume material featuring less common sexual practices,
including sadomasochistic and violent sexual behaviors.
He also noted that after frequent exposure to pornography,
'Erections were less pronounced and more poorly maintained.'
Viewing more extreme porn was thus appealing because it was
still capable of producing sexual excitedness. However, the
introduction of novel porn failed to return interest to initial
levels. Pleasure reactions were flat or indicated disappointment
and this lack of responsiveness lingered for weeks, but did
gradually improve.[31]

In short, more than 25 year ago, there was already evidence
that porn video viewers tended toward habituation, declining
sexual responsiveness, a need for more extreme visual stimuli
and dissatisfaction. Today's highspeed porn exploits this innate
vulnerability by permitting rapid, limitless escalation.

A second reason porn tastes can escalate is tolerance, which
is a more lasting addiction process that drives a need for greater

and greater stimulation. As we'll see in the next chapter, sexual novelty is a sure-fire way to bring your flagging member back to attention. If a new porn star won't do it, try gang rape or gore. No, you wouldn't rape or dismember anyone, but you may now need extreme material and underlying anxiety to get you going. As you may recall from the introduction, psychiatrist Norman Doidge also observed this process in his patients.

This phenomenon is so common, and evidence of recovery so reassuring, that I'll share a range of self-reports:

> *As my porn use progressed throughout college, I slowly fell prey to more and more hardcore shit, like really weird shit, that is now no longer turning me on when I think about it. This is one of the greatest feelings of all – to know that my fantasies are returning to those of a normal, earth-born and bred, human being.*

*

> *I'm tired of hearing, 'You like what you like' from people. A lot of the things I look at I don't like. I just can't get off to the normal stuff anymore. I never thought I'd wank to girls pissing on each other – and now it doesn't do it for me anymore. Sexuality is tricky and I think we've only begun to look at the effects that internet porn has on human beings. All of us are test subjects and from what I've read over and over, people are noticing changes.*

*

> *I can say with absolute certainty that the fantasies I had about rape, homicide and submission were never there before hardcore porn use from 18-22. When I stayed away from porn for 5 months all those fantasies and urges were gone. My natural sexual taste was vanilla again and still is. Thing with porn is you need harder and harder material, more taboo, more exciting and 'wrong' to actually be able to get off.*

*

I never thought that I'd be able to have normal sex. I always thought that my brain was just hard-wired to only be turned on by my femdom fetish [female-domination porn that humiliates men], similar to the way a gay guy can only be turned on by cock and cannot appreciate sex with a woman. Little did I know that the fetish I thought was hard-wired, was simply the result of my porn-viewing habits. It was a hell of my own making. After 3 months of no porn, my latest sexual encounter has removed any doubt about the effectiveness of quitting.

*

I'm a 23-year old male in good physical condition. I started high-speed porn at 15, quickly escalating from normal porn to bukkake porn [repeated ejaculation on a female by many men], transgender porn, femdom porn, incest, etc. I didn't realize how much I was hurting myself until I lost my virginity at 20 and had problems achieving and maintaining an erection. It seriously hurt my self-confidence and made me fearful of sex. Similar results with other women. I kept increasing the frequency and length of porn sessions, and escalating to more disturbing fetishes. After a year, I tried to have sex with an attractive girl. I couldn't perform. I spiralled down a hole of despair. I started watching sissy hypno porn, and occasionally anal masturbation. I thought I might have turned gay, but gay porn never did it for me. I found NoFap and quit. After a few relapses, I made my 90-day mark. I have lost my cravings for all porn, especially extreme porn. At 87 days, I had my first date in ages. At 96 days, my first BJ [fellatio] since quitting. No problems at all, which is amazing because I used to get bored during BJs and lose my erection. And at 113 days, I had sex and performed better than ever, with a rock-hard erection the whole time. I feel like I've been given a second chance at life.

*

*As any porn junkie knows, the more porn you watch, the more you need and the more hardcore porn you need to feel fully aroused. At my worst I was dabbling in bestiality, frequent incest scenes, or other hardcore porn. Actual vaginal sex was never too arousing for me. Oral or other types of non-vaginal sex were **way** more appealing. They made the woman just a pleasure-giving object. After months of 'mental detox', if you will, and multiple real-life partners, I've lost my fixation to alternative types of sex. I'm actually attracted to vaginas now. Sounds funny, doesn't it? I still enjoy other types of sex on occasion, but the intimacy of being inside of a woman is second-to-none. Seriously, it's way, way more sexy now. This is obviously a win-win in real life. And my urge to watch porn went from a constant roar to an occasional whimper. This is not an exaggeration.*

Men have long believed that what arouses them to orgasm is ironclad evidence of their sexual orientation. Therefore, it can be especially distressing to escalate through shifting porn fetishes that ultimately cast doubt on sexual orientation. Yet such escalation to unexpected tastes is surprisingly common today, especially among young people who grew up dabbling in 'anything-goes' tube sites from an early age:

When I got internet back in my late teens I found many YouTube-like porn sites that categorized content by fetishes. At first my tastes were those of a normal teenage boy, but over the years my tastes shifted into aggressive content. Violent themes against women to be more specific, especially those anime/hentai videos with scenarios too vile to portray in real life. Eventually I got bored of that stuff, and in my 20s found new stuff. Within a year I had acquired many new fetishes, each changing within a shorter time frame than the one before it. I'm experimenting with quitting because

> *my tastes are now making me really uncomfortable. They conflict with my sexuality.*

Worse yet, there's a widespread meme online that internet porn is enabling users to 'discover their sexuality'. Some bold young explorers industriously seek out the hottest material they can find in the belief that it reveals who they are sexually. They don't realize that a boner isn't the only measure of a person's fundamental sexual proclivities.

For example, the addiction process itself can drive escalation to more extreme material, while making porn that used to seem hot appear confusingly unexciting. Also, anxiety-producing material pumps up sexual arousal.[32] As one researcher explained, a quickening pulse, dilating pupils and clammy skin – the body's reaction to adrenaline – can be mistaken for sexual attraction. 'We misinterpret our arousal. It is an error of presumption'.[33] A review of existing research confirms that sexual interests are conditionable (changeable),[34] and different from fundamental sexual orientation.[35]

By following their erections from genre to genre, some young users migrate to content that they feel is at odds with their sexual identity:

> *I'm gay but porn can get me sexually interested in females. Well ... not breasts, but the other female parts become arousing. Porn is an overly charged erotic atmosphere. All inhibitions are down and the desire for arousal becomes dominant.*

> *

> *As the years slipped by gonzo simply wouldn't do it anymore. Recently, I actually looked at gay porn because I was bored. It was like, here I am, 28, and I've seen all the porn on the internet essentially, so I might as well look at gay porn. That moment the seed was planted, 'This is seriously f--ked, you need to stop this'. Of course I didn't then.*

*

Reddit and the Empty Closets forum are full of people, gay/bi/straight, who are completely lost and confused about their orientation and freaking out about why they want to suck cocks or watch weird stuff after use of porn. The highspeed generation's porn users are going online and asking for answers. On French forums it's the same. Thousands of people posting, and so many don't know why they developed penis fetishes or femdom addiction. The common factor is internet use (porn, chat, dating sites).

When users become obsessed with sexual-orientation doubts they refer to it as SOCD or HOCD, that is, 'sexual-orientation (or homosexual) obsessive-compulsive disorder':

(Age 19) I seriously thought I was turning gay. My HOCD was so strong at that time, I was contemplating taking a dive off the nearest high-rise. I felt so depressed. I knew I loved girls and I can't love another dude, but why did I have ED? Why did I need transgender/gay stuff to shock me into arousal?

Let me emphasise that it is not only heterosexuals who become anxious about their sexual orientation due to escalation to new porn genres:

I myself had HOCD, in the sense that I feared myself to actually be heterosexual, since I eventually was exclusively turned on by straight and 'lesbian' porn. Yes, 'feared,' because my entire social identity was as a gay man and I am married to a man. If I went 'back to straight' – a move that nobody would ever believe and is more taboo nowadays than coming out as gay – I would be a social outcast. Finally, I realized that I had eroticized the fear itself.

Any form of OCD is potentially a serious medical disorder. Whether you are gay, straight or undecided, if you have these symptoms, seek help from a healthcare professional who thoroughly understands that OCD is a compulsion to check constantly to reassure yourself, and who won't jump to the conclusion that you are in denial about your sexuality.

I went to a psychiatrist. He confirmed I have OCD and he prescribed alprazolam (Xanax). Now, my symptoms of HOCD are very, very mild. I can think way clearer. It improved my appetite and I've had some of the best sleep of my life. Also, now I know I am not gay or bi, and my withdrawal from porn has become a lot easier because my anxiety has dropped. So, if someone asks you, 'How serious is porn addiction?' say that you know a guy who had to get on Xanax in order to make it through the withdrawal.

Loss of attraction to real partners

'Young Japanese men are growing indifferent or even averse to sex, while married couples are starting to have it even less,' reported the *Japan Times*, citing a 2010 poll that revealed a striking trend. More than 36% of men aged 16 to 19 had no interest in sex, more than double the 17.5 % from 2008. Men between 20 and 24 showed a similar trend, jumping from 11.8 % to 21.5 %, while men between 45 and 49 leaped from 8.7 % to 22.1 %.[36] Japan isn't alone. In France, a 2008 survey found that 20 percent of younger French men had no interest in sex.[37]

Something peculiar is afoot, and it has invaded the States as well. In a 2014 study, young men who viewed a lot of porn were more likely to rely on it to become and remain aroused and more likely to use it during partnered sexual activities. In addition, they enjoyed sex less than men who use less porn.[38]

It is not unusual for people on porn recovery forums to ask the question, 'Do you think I am asexual?' When asked if they masturbate, the answer is usually, 'Yes, 2-3 times a day to porn'. Are they asexual or just hooked on porn? Its never-ending stimulation can provide a buzz long after real-life partners begin to pale.

I'm not asexual strictly speaking, as I still find women beautiful. But I'm no longer attracted to them, either sexually or romantically, though I consciously know they are attractive. Do you guys get that painful feeling when you look at a hot girl? You would like to be turned on but you just can't. It makes me angry.

*

(Age 18) Before starting porn at 15 I was EXTREMELY horny and would chase anything on 2 legs. I made out with girls and got insane boners. After porn ruined me, I was completely disinterested in girls and could never maintain an erection. At my young age I knew there was something definitely wrong with me because I'm supposed to be women-crazy like I used to be before porn. At 17 I began my reboot. Yesterday I successfully had sex with no ED drugs and my boner was amazing.

*

There's a new orb of light surrounding women. They're just beautiful, and cute, and playful. And yeah I love to look at them and admire their beauty and sexiness, because we're guys; that's what we do. But it's so much more than that. It's almost indescribable how stopping using porn has made me value woman and the time I spend with them in so much more of a wholesome way. After years of fapping 5-12x per week to pornography, sex was embarrassing. Not only was there not enough friction but it felt like the 'wrong' type of stimulation. Six months later I have no performance issues of any kind. Sex is now 20x more fulfilling than masturbation.

It takes foreplay for me to reach my peak arousal now and my partners absolutely love that. I laugh at myself when I fap on occasion and am left a bit disappointed.

*

(Age 19) For years, I thought I used porn because I was horny. I thought that if I could get a girl to have sex with me, I wouldn't have to fap. But I recently passed up having sex with a woman I work with twice! *And then I f--king went home and fapped while fantasising about having sex with her. The most messed up thing about this is that I didn't realize how f--ked up this was until yesterday. I mean, if I had actually been fapping because I wanted to have sex, I would have just gone through with it, right? I was in denial.*

*

(Day 46) For the last three days I have felt that strong, natural sexual attraction to real women while out and about. I just naturally notice a woman's figure and it turns me on without me having to think about it. Duh, that's how it's supposed to work! Damn, it's amazing how porn screws you up! My penile sensitivity has been off the charts, too. I honestly don't remember ever feeling like this.

*

I'm known as the 'unrealistic-high-standards-on-chicks' guy among my friends, yet I hardly score. After 40 days, I'm approaching more girls than ever, not -only- for their looks, but the way they are and what they talk about. Before, girls weren't special. They were 'just ok'. My brain wanted unrealistic whores, and it's just now that I've realised how many years I wasted chasing fantasy relations instead of being happy with what life was giving me (which, in hindsight, were some of the nicest girls I've met). Yet I continued the useless search...

*

In the past I noticed beauty, of course, but never FELT a DESIRE to be with a girl. I directed all my sex drive toward porn. Everything sexual for me WAS porn. I could never think about me, this guy with this cock, having real sex with a real girl. Now, I feel like sex is the most natural thing to do. 'Hell yeah it's possible for me to have sex. Hell yeah there's a lot of girls out there wanting to have it with me!' Suddenly, self-defeating thoughts seem so stupid and time-wasting. I finally feel what most males feel. And it's awesome.

Effects on libido, romance

Relationships, too, are affected by porn use, which makes sense. Too much stimulation can interfere with what scientists call pair-bonding, or falling in love. When scientists jacked up pair-bonding animals on amphetamine, the naturally monogamous animals no longer formed a preference for one partner.[39] The artificial stimulation hijacks their bonding machinery, leaving them just like regular (promiscuous) mammals – in which the brain circuits for lasting bonds are absent.

Research in humans also suggests that too much stimulation weakens pair bonds. According to a 2007 study, mere exposure to numerous sexy female images causes a man to devalue his real-life partner.[40] He rates her lower not only on attractiveness, but also on warmth and intelligence. Also, after pornography consumption, subjects of both sexes report less satisfaction with their intimate partner – including the partner's affection, appearance, sexual curiosity and performance.[41] And both men and women assign increased importance to sex without emotional involvement.

(Day 125) I am in a long-term relationship, and I can vouch for the fact that quitting helped our sex life. A lot. I had no ED or PE or any other kind of sex-related problems,

but compared to what we have now, our sex life while I was fapping was .... dull. Now it is anything but dull, and both of us have stronger libidos than before. I am not exactly sure how – or if – my quitting affected **her** *libido, but she sure is much more interested in sex now :).*

*

(Age 50) Over the years, I suggested to my wife various activities straight out of porn stories. She was okay with some of them, but it never satisfied at all. Although we had a decent sex life relative to most people our age, I was always comparing the porn scenarios with my real life and real wife and feeling dissatisfied. Now, things are shifting. During intercourse last night, I felt suddenly very intimate, almost scarily intimate, deep contact I have never experienced before. It felt kind of shocking to me. It was wonderful in a way I can't describe, but I am in a kind of awe over it.

*

(Age 19) Even though I watched porn I was never really one to want sex. TWO guys managed to grab my interest. However, I think porn/masturbation was suppressing my longing to be with either of them. Since quitting, I suddenly had this intense realization that I really like those two, and I could see myself completely happy in a committed relationship with either. Suddenly it felt like...my heart was reaching out for them. Instead of daydreaming, my body was like, 'Let's go make this happen in real life.' All of a sudden I felt this huge wave of some weird attraction-type energy surge over me. [He soon began a relationship with one of the men.]

*

(Age 30) In the past, sex wasn't emotional. On some level it was like nobody else was there because I was in my own

head the whole time for one reason or another (fantasizing, DE issues, etc...). Girlfriends during my mid 20's to early 30's just didn't arouse me anywhere close to what high-speed porn offered, no matter how good they looked. I didn't recognize these things at the time of course, but since beginning this journey 4 months ago, I can honestly say I'm shocked how good sex can be with your girlfriend when you eliminate the constant, steady pattern of porn use.

*

(200 days) I now have an undeniable sex drive. I want my wife more than ever. If a long time passes without sex, I feel this thing called 'sexual tension', which is apparently real. I notice things I never noticed before. Hair tossing, quick glances, breathing patterns, body language. It is a different world. And let me tell you – when you get to this point, you really won't care about whatever super-specific porno fetishes you thought were the only thing you could get off to, because just the word WOMAN (or man or whatever) will make you feel urges.

*

(Day 90) My bad habit of seeing only the beauty in women automatically shifted. Right now I want to go out there and find a mate. My sexual desire has never been higher, and I'm more observant towards women who could become good girlfriends and eventually good mothers. It's not entirely about their beauty anymore.

*

Before realizing that porn was the problem, I used to think I needed to get healthier fantasies. Now, almost 8 months after quitting porn, I'm finding that the fantasies I used to have don't appeal to me anymore...at all. What I found is that my wife and I both enjoy sex much, much more when there is no fantasy involved; just the two of us in the moment. I'm now able to make love to her without erectile issues, face-to-face with eye contact.

Social anxiety, self-esteem

As users manage to abstain from porn, their desire to connect with others generally surges. Often, so does their self-esteem, their ability to look others in the eye, their sense of humour, their optimism, their attractiveness to potential mates, and so forth. Even those formerly suffering from severe social anxiety often explore new avenues for social contact: smiling and joking with work colleagues, online dating, meditation groups, joining clubs, nightspots, and so forth. In some cases it takes months, but for others the shift is so rapid that it catches them by surprise.

YBOP wasn't alone in chronicling this unexpected connection. In his famous TED talk "The Demise of Guys", well known psychologist Phillip Zimbardo noted that 'arousal addiction' (porn, video games) is a major factor in the increase in social awkwardness and anxiety among digital natives.

Zimbardo's hypothesis is that excessive screen time interferes with development of normal social skills. Clearly this is so.[42] [43] However, this doesn't explain the increase in confidence and extraversion after quitting, or why some guys improve so quickly.

In *The Brain That Changes Itself*, psychiatrist Norman Doidge suggests that the intense stimulation of today's porn hijacks and rewires 'brain real estate' that would otherwise be devoted to making social ties rewarding. Real people become less rewarding; fake people become far more enticing. Perhaps removing porn re-opens the space for natural rewards such as friends and partners. In the next chapter, I'll highlight the specific brain changes that help account for the link between social anxiety and porn use:

Now that I look back at my life there has ALWAYS been

connection between porn consumption, masturbation and my social anxiety. Before porn, I had a lot of friends, a couple of girlfriends, and I felt like I was on the top of the world. There was nothing that could bring me down. I felt like I had my own way to react to everything that could happen. Then I got a new computer... After a year or two I found myself in REALLY deep social anxiety, combined with too much pot and nothing interesting to do with my life.

*

I'm not your generic self-diagnosed socially awkward penguin. I've been to a psychiatrist, diagnosed with moderate to severe social-anxiety and was put on medication. I know about the adrenaline rush you get when a stranger gets near you, the almost heart attack you feel when you try to talk during a class or a meeting (as if you ever do), the long lonely walks you take not to deal with strangers, the unfounded shame when you look another person in the eye, the huge wall you put between strangers. Sweating, trembling, panic attacks, self hate, suicidal impulses, I've been through it all. I've been attempting quitting for two years now and this is the longest I've abstained. I no longer experience the 'torture' I described above. No I'm not a new person, not a social butterfly. I'm still myself but I'm free of the shackles we call social phobia. In this past two years I've made more connections, hit on more women, made more friends than I did in my first 25 years. I feel content and comfortable in my own skin, and the wall I put between myself and other people has crumbled.

*

Social interaction. I was completely afraid of it and incapable of it 50 days ago. In the past week or so, I have interacted incredibly smoothly and effortlessly with people with whom I would have been unable to interact with while using. I used to be unable to look people in the eyes. I used to purposefully hide from people I knew in public so as to avoid awkward conversation. I wasn't able to be invested in the conversation. Women, even those I knew personally, would intimidate me. I would fantasize throughout the day about being able to interact like a normal human... All of this is now changing before my eyes in a most drastic way. I can interact with confidence; be myself. I can hold an unbreakable gaze into other people's eyes. I am actually part of the conversation, as opposed to being aloof and thinking about leaving it.

New people I meet tell me they like my confidence and they think I'm a good speaker, compliments I would've never expected to hear just a few months ago.

*

My interactions with females are completely transformed. It seems there is some unconscious recognition that you have more power or something. It's hard to explain. Females are complimenting me on my looks and body. My awareness around social situations is much better. I can read people's body language better. People cannot intimidate me as before. I feel that their anger just bounces off me, and I stay in a serene state.

Inability to concentrate

Those who reboot commonly report that they have 'better concentration', 'no more brain fog', 'clearer thinking' and 'improved memory'. Addiction neuroscientists have repeatedly shown that internet addiction produces memory, concentration and impulse-control problems in some users, as well as corresponding brain changes.[44] For example, researchers found that the severity of ADHD symptoms correlates with the severity of internet addiction, even when they take into account anxiety, depression and personality traits.[36] And, as we'll see later, German researchers recently confirmed that moderate porn use, even by non-addicts, correlates with shrunken grey matter in regions of the brain associated with cognitive function.[46]

When I was [using internet porn] I had brain fog or a constant hung-over-like feeling, which made it hard for me to concentrate, talk to people or just do my everyday tasks. After 7-10 days without porn this feeling went away. My mind became very clear, thoughts easily controllable, and I became much more relaxed in general.

*

I am 34 and went on Adderall for the first time a few months ago. 2 months after quitting porn, I really don't even need it anymore. Some of the benefits I have experienced: I can retain and remember information a lot better. I remember events in my past life a lot better. I am not irritable, and am more focused. I can execute tasks a lot faster.

*

Another result: my writing is much better. I don't mean handwriting (though that got better too). I mean word choice, sentence structure, etc. During my first year of graduate school (which I just finished), writing was a real chore. Now, after no-porn, it's a pleasure. So easy and free. I have more words at my disposal, probably because my memory has improved in general.

*

Memory – I always had a good one, but quitting put it

through the roof. I could enter a room of 15 people and learn
+ recall specifically all their phone numbers in under 5 min.
Marks perfect. Social anxiety and BS negative thinking – >
out with the trash.

*

For those of you who are in uni, NoFap is a miracle for the
brain. Before, I used to have to force myself to concentrate
in class and would still end up 'zoning out'. Now, I can
concentrate in a 3-hour lecture with almost no issues (it's
still improving).

Depression, low energy, discouragement

Scientists now view depression as a condition of low energy
and little motivation. Recent research confirmed that the 'go
get it!' neurochemical dopamine is the main player.[47] In fact,
impaired/restored dopamine signalling may be behind many
of the symptoms/improvements reported by recovering users.
Again, I'll have a lot more to say about that in the next chapter:

I'm finding I experience depression and feelings of
worthlessness far less often. I'm able to get up more easily
in the morning and find the motivation to do the bloody
dishes more often before going to bed.

*

I'm happier. Much, much happier. I typically suffer from
SAD and was diagnosed with minor clinical depression a
few years back, but this autumn/winter I'm feeling great. I
have more energy.

*

As a man with genetic depression, being porn free has done
more for me than any drugs I have ever had to take. It is

as if this makes me more alert, attentive, and happier than
Wellbutrin, Zoloft or the other drugs I was cycled through.

*

I finally have energy again! I haven't felt this good since
secondary school. It's not like I'm Hulk or anything, but I
finally have extra energy to DO stuff. I spent most of my
early 20's in a state of low energy and mild depression. I
attribute like 80% of it to the fact that I was using porn
twice a day. Now that I've stopped, I've been exercising,
being more social, and generally enjoying life.

*

Before I had anxiety, depression, was always lazy. It was a
struggle to get out and face the day. Avoided a lot of social
situations unless I was drunk. Now, I have tons of energy.
When I look in the mirror I feel like my skin has a glow to
it. I joined a gym and started lifting weights, my lifts have
been progressing like crazy. I run at least 2k a day right when
I wake up. Social situations are a breeze. When walking
around in public I feel so powerful, like I can talk to anyone
and do anything. I have noticed girls checking me out.

*

Quitting isn't a cure all for your life problems – but it's the
foundation, a ploughed field in which you can sow seeds for
a new future that isn't bedevilled by the secrecy and shame
that comes with falling into the seemingly inescapable pit
of porn-related despair that so many of us know. A life of
hope and strength – not jizzy tissues, jealousy, bitterness,
self-hatred, resentment and unfulfilled dreams.

In the light of this vast, informal experiment, it seems clear that
the widely held view of clinicians that pornography, specifically
online pornography, is harmless should be reconsidered as
a matter of urgency. We can't be sure that the thousands of

people describing their recovery from excessive porn use are mistaken.

As we'll see next, it is quite plausible that the symptoms they describe are real, that online pornography use causes them, and that behavioural change can bring significant benefits. In any case, porn users suffering from the kinds of symptoms outlined above have little to lose from cutting out internet porn for a few months to see if their symptoms resolve.

2

Wanting Run Amok

Choice is a subtle form of disease.

Don DeLillo, *Running Dog*

Ever heard of the Coolidge effect? It's a graphic example of how unrelentingly sexual novelty can drive behaviour. The effect shows up in mammals ranging from rams to rats, and here's how it works: Drop a male rat into a cage with a receptive female rat. First, you see a frenzy of copulation. Then, progressively, the male tires of that particular female. Even if she wants more, he has had enough.

However, replace the original female with a fresh one, and the male immediately revives and gallantly struggles to fertilize *her*. You can repeat this process with fresh females until he is completely wiped out. Reproduction, after all, is genes' top priority. Just ask Australia's mouse-like antechinus, which engages in such a furious mating frenzy that it destroys its own immune system and drops dead.

Obviously, human mating is generally more complex. For one thing we're among the peculiar 3 to 5 percent of mammals with the capacity for long-term bonds. Yet sexual novelty can enthral us too.

The Coolidge effect itself gets its name from US President Calvin Coolidge. He and his wife were touring a farm. While the president was elsewhere, the farmer proudly showed Mrs. Coolidge a rooster that could copulate with hens all day long, day after day. Mrs. Coolidge coyly suggested that the farmer tell that to Mr. Coolidge, which he did. The president thought for a moment and then enquired, 'With the same hen?'

'No, sir,' replied the farmer.

'Tell that to Mrs. Coolidge,' retorted the president.

An appreciation for a fine novel partner helps propel internet porn use. At its most fundamental level, this impulse is evolution's way of discouraging inbreeding and keeping the gene pool as fresh as possible. What powers the lure of novelty at the physical level? Dopamine.

Primitive circuits in the brain govern emotions, drives, impulses, and subconscious decision-making.[48] They do their jobs so efficiently that evolution hasn't seen the need to change them much since before humans were human.[49] The desire and motivation to pursue sex arises from a neurochemical called dopamine.[50] Dopamine amps up the centrepiece of a primitive part of the brain known as the reward circuitry. It's where you experience cravings and pleasure *and* where you get addicted.

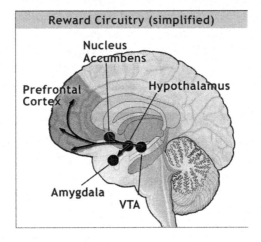

This ancient reward circuitry compels you to do things that further your survival and pass on your genes. At the top of our human reward list are food,[51] sex,[52] love,[53] friendship, and novelty.[54] These are called 'natural reinforcers,' as contrasted with addictive chemicals (which can hijack this same circuitry).

The evolutionary purpose of dopamine is to motivate you to do what serves your genes.[55] The bigger the squirt the more you want something. No dopamine and you just ignore it. High-calorie chocolate cake and ice cream – a big blast. Celery – not so much. Dopamine surges are the barometer by which you determine the value of any experience. They tell you what to approach or avoid, and where to put your attention. Further, dopamine tells you what to remember by helping to rewire your brain.[56] Sexual stimulation and orgasm add up to the biggest natural blast of dopamine available to your reward circuitry.

Although dopamine is sometimes referred to as the 'pleasure molecule', it is actually about seeking and searching[57] for pleasure, *not* pleasure itself. Thus dopamine rises with anticipation.[58] It's your motivation and drive to pursue potential pleasure or long term goals.[59] It works in the synapses of nerve cells by attaching to receptors to stimulate electrical impulses, as pictured here.

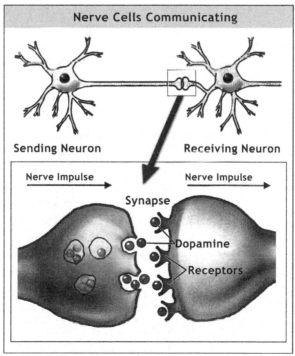

Nerve Cells Communicating

Sending Neuron   Receiving Neuron

Nerve Impulse →   Nerve Impulse →

Synapse

Dopamine

Receptors

The pleasure of climax appears to arise from opioids, so think of dopamine as *wanting* and opioids as *liking*.[60] As psychologist Susan Weinschenk explained,[61] 'dopamine causes us to want, desire, seek out, and search'. Yet 'the dopamine system is stronger than the opioid system. We seek more than we are satisfied. ... Seeking is more likely to keep us alive than sitting around in a satisfied stupor.'

Addiction may be thought of as *wanting run amok*.[62]

Novelty, Novelty, More Novelty

Dopamine surges for novelty.[63] A new vehicle, just-released film, the latest gadget…we are all hooked on dopamine. As with everything new the thrill fades away as dopamine plummets. So, as in the example above, the rat's reward circuitry is squirting less and less dopamine with respect to the current female, but produces a big dopamine surge for a new female.

Does this sound familiar? When Australian researchers displayed the same erotic film repeatedly, test subjects' penises and subjective reports both revealed a progressive decrease in sexual arousal.[64] The 'same old same old' just gets boring. Habituation indicates declining dopamine. After 18 viewings – just as the test subjects were nodding off – researchers introduced novel erotica for the 19th and 20th viewings (see graph opposite). Bingo! The subjects and their penises sprang to attention. (Yes, women showed similar effects.[65])

Internet porn is especially enticing to the reward circuitry because novelty is always just a click away. It could be a novel 'mate', unusual scene, strange sexual act, or – you fill in the blank. And the most popular sites – the so-called tube sites – build this pursuit of novelty into their layout. Every page presents dozens of different clips and genres to choose from. They are engrossing precisely because they offer what seems like inexhaustible novelty.

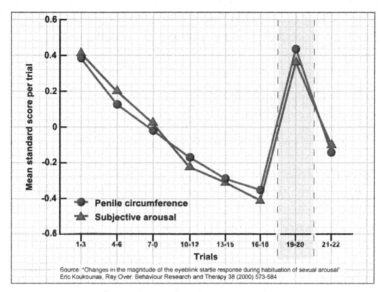

Source: "Changes in the magnitude of the eyeblink startle response during habituation of sexual arousal"
Eric Koukounas, Ray Over. Behaviour Research and Therapy 38 (2000) 573-584

With multiple tabs open and clicking for hours, you can 'experience' more novel sex partners every ten minutes than your hunter-gatherer ancestors experienced in a lifetime. Of course the reality is different. What feels like a cornucopia of riches is only countless hours spent in front of a screen, seeking something that exists elsewhere.

I always opened several windows in my browser, each one with many, many tabs. The main thing that arouses me is novelty. New faces, new bodies, new 'choices'. I very rarely even watched a whole porn scene, and can't remember when I saw an entire movie. Too boring. I always wanted NEW stuff.

Supernormal Stimulus

Erotic words, pictures and videos have been around a long time –as has the neurochemical rush from novel mates. So what makes today's porn uniquely compelling? Not just its unending novelty. Dopamine fires up for other emotions and stimuli too, all of which often feature prominently in internet porn:

- Surprise,[66] shock (What *isn't* shocking in today's porn?)

- Anxiety[67] (Using porn that isn't consistent with your values or sexuality.)

- Seeking[68] and searching (Wanting, anticipating)

In fact, internet porn looks very much like what scientists call a supernormal stimulus.[69] Years ago, Nobel laureate Nikolaas Tinbergen discovered that birds, butterflies, and other animals could be duped into preferring fake eggs and mates. Female birds, for example, struggled to sit on Tinbergen's larger-than-life, vividly spotted plaster eggs while their own pale, dappled eggs perished untended. Male jewel beetles will ignore real mates in favour of futile efforts to copulate with the dimpled brown bottoms of beer bottles.[70] To a beetle, a beer bottle lying on the ground looks like the biggest, most beautiful, sexiest female he has ever seen.

In other words, instead of the instinctive response stopping at a 'sweet spot' where it doesn't lure the animal out of the mating game entirely, this innate programming continues to trigger enthusiastic responses to unrealistic, synthetic stimuli. Tinbergen dubbed such deceptions 'supranormal stimuli,' although they are now often referred to simply as 'supernormal stimuli'.

Supernormal stimuli are exaggerated versions of normal stimuli that we falsely perceive as valuable. Interestingly, although it's unlikely a monkey would choose images over real mates, monkeys will 'pay' (forego juice rewards) to view images of female monkey bottoms.[71] Perhaps it's not so surprising that today's porn can hijack our instincts.

When we make an artificial supernormal stimulus our top priority it's because it has triggered a bigger blast of dopamine in our brain's reward circuit than its natural counterpart. For most users, yesteryear's porn magazines couldn't compete with real partners. A *Playboy* centrefold did not duplicate the other cues earlier porn users had learned to associate with real potential or actual partners: eye contact, touch, scent, the thrill of flirting and dancing, foreplay, sex and so forth.

Today's internet porn, however, is laced with supernormal stimulation. First, it offers endless novel hotties available at a click. Research confirms that anticipation of reward and novelty amplify one another to increase excitement and rewire the reward circuitry of the brain.[72]

Second, internet porn offers countless artificially enhanced breasts and Viagra-sustained gargantuan penises, exaggerated grunts of desire, pile-driving thrusts, double or triple penetration, gang-bangs and other unrealistic scenarios.

Third, for most people, static images cannot compare with today's hi-def 3-minute videos of people engaged in intense sex. With stills of naked bunnies all you had was your own imagination. You always knew what was going to happen next, which wasn't much in the case of a pre-internet 13-year old. In contrast, with an endless stream of 'I can't believe what I just saw' videos, your expectations are constantly violated (which the brain finds more stimulating).[73] Keep in mind also, that humans evolved to learn by watching others doing things, so videos are more powerful 'how to' lessons than stills.

With science-fiction weirdness that would have made Tinbergen say, 'I told you so', today's porn users often find internet erotica more stimulating than real partners. Users might not want to spend hours hunched in front of a computer staring at porn and compulsively clicking on new images. They might prefer to spend time socialising with friends and meeting potential partners in the process. Yet reality struggles to compete at the level of the brain's response, especially when one throws into the balance the uncertainties and reversals of social interaction. As Noah Church puts it in his memoir

Wack: Addicted to Internet Porn, 'it's not that I didn't want real sex, it's just that it was so much harder and more confusing to pursue than pornography.' And this finds an echo in numerous first person accounts:

> *I went through a period of being single, stuck in a small town where there were very few dating opportunities, and I began to masturbate frequently with porn. I was amazed at how quickly I got sucked in. I began losing days of work surfing porn sites. And yet I didn't fully appreciate what was happening to me until I was in bed with a woman and caught myself furiously trying to recall an exciting porn image in order to get hard. I did not imagine that it could happen to me. Fortunately, I had a long foundation of healthy sex before porn and I recognized what was going on. After I quit, I started getting laid again, and often. And shortly after that I met my wife.*

These days, there's no end of supernormal stimulation in sight. The porn industry already offers 3-D porn and robots[74] and sex toys synchronized with porn[75] or other computer users to simulate physical action.[76] But danger lurks when something:

– registers as an especially 'valuable', that is, exaggerated version of a thing that our ancestors (and we) evolved to find irresistible (high-calorie food, sexual arousal),

– is available conveniently in limitless supply (not found in nature),

– comes in lots of varieties (abundant novelty),

– and we chronically overconsume it.

Cheap, plentiful junk food fits this model and is universally recognized as a supernormal stimulus. You can slam down a 32-ounce soft drink and a bag of salty nibbles without much thought, but just try to consume their caloric equivalent in dried venison and boiled roots!

Similarly, viewers routinely spend hours surfing galleries of porn videos searching for the right video to finish, keeping dopamine elevated for abnormally long periods. But try to envision a hunter-gatherer routinely spending the same number of hours masturbating to the same stick-figure on a cave wall. Didn't happen.

Porn poses unique risks beyond supernormal stimulation. First, it's easy to access, available 24/7, free and private. Second, most users start watching porn by puberty, when their brain's are at their peak of plasticity and most vulnerable to addiction and rewiring.

Finally, there are limits on food consumption: stomach capacity and the natural aversion that kicks in when we can't face one more bite of something. In contrast, there are *no* physical limits on internet porn consumption, other than the need for sleep and bathroom breaks. A user can edge (masturbate without climaxing) to porn for hours without triggering feelings of satiation, or aversion.

Bingeing on porn feels like a promise of pleasure, but recall that the message of dopamine isn't 'satisfaction'. It's, 'keep going, satisfaction is j-u-s-t around the corner':

I would arouse myself close to orgasm then stop, keep watching porn, and stay at medium levels, always edging. I was more concerned with watching the porn than getting to orgasm. Porn had me locked in focus until eventually I was just exhausted and orgasmed out of surrender.

Unwanted Adaptation: Sexual Conditioning and Addiction

What's a brain to do when it has unlimited access to a super-stimulating reward it never evolved to handle? Some brains adapt – and not in a good way. The process is gradual. At first, using porn and masturbating to orgasm resolves sexual tension and registers as satisfying.

But if you chronically overstimulate yourself, your brain may start to work against you. It protects itself against excessive stimulation by reducing dopamine signaling, and you feel less and less gratified.[77] As you can see in this image, the brain accomplishes this by reducing dopamine receptors and releasing less dopamine, pushing some users into an even more determined search for stimulation. These physical brain changes lead to desensitisation, which drives the need for greater stimulation (tolerance). They can be challenging to reverse. As one user said, 'Porn goes in like a needle but comes out like a fishhook.'

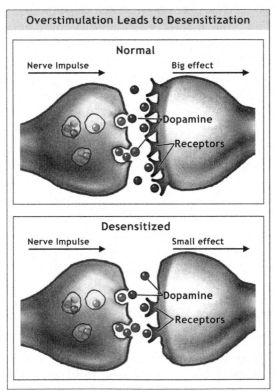

Sexual Conditioning

One possible outcome is unanticipated sexual conditioning – which didn't happen to your father when he used *Playboy*. Perhaps you wire your sexual excitement to a screen, constant novelty, voyeurism or bizarre acts. Worst case, you eventually need both porn's content and delivery-at-a-click to sustain arousal.

> *Before I quit I had the utmost trouble getting off. I actually had to close my eyes and imagine a CONSTANT stream of porn to climax. I was more or less using my girlfriends' bodies to help me jerk off. After a long streak without porn, I could climax easily, without thinking about it. It was a miracle. It was the best feeling ever.*

Most news stories about youthful porn use focus on conscious learning. The assumption is that all we need to tell teens is that porn isn't like real sex and all will be well.[78] This remedy ignores the *unconscious* effects of porn viewing.

At the same time young Jamie is consciously learning that women 'love' ejaculate on their faces, he may unconsciously be learning that ejaculating on women's faces is sexually arousing. This kind of unconscious learning happens to some degree every time he finds porn exciting.[79] Of course, what turns Jamie on at 14 may bear no relation to what he's watching at 16. He may have graduated to femdom or incest porn.

Superficial conditioning (or learning) can be summed up as, 'So this is how people have sex and this is how *I* should do it.' Unconscious sexual conditioning can be summed up as, 'This is what turns me on' or, at a brain level, 'This is what jacks up my dopamine'. It could be as simple as preferring redheads. Or maybe dainty feet or pecs appeal more than breasts.

However our preferences arise, our brains evolved to record what turns us on. This phenomenon rests on a crucial neural principle: *Nerve cells that fire together wire together.* Briefly, the brain links together the nerve cells for sexual excitement (in the reward circuit) with the nerve cells that store memories of the events associated with the excitement. For example, type in your favourite porn site and you activate nerve cells that blast your reward circuitry. Up goes your dopamine. Repeated activity strengthens the connections between nerve cells as pictured.

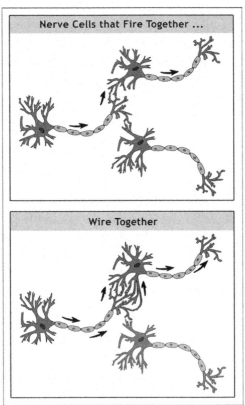

Brains are plastic, and once you wire up a new cue you have no way of knowing when it will trigger a future reaction. Much as Pavlov's dog learned to salivate to the bell, today's porn users learn to wire unexpected stimuli to their erections. The brain's primitive reward circuitry isn't aware that the bell isn't food, or that the novel porn isn't 'my' porn. Its axiom is simply 'Dopamine *good*'.

In 2004 Swedish researchers found that 99% of young men had consumed pornography. That's ancient history in terms of porn's delivery, yet more than half felt it had had an impact on their sexual behaviour.[80]

Even if you're watching tame porn and haven't developed any porn-induced fetishes, the issue of *how* you get your jollies can have repercussions. If you use internet porn, you may be training yourself for the role of voyeur or to need the option of clicking to something more arousing at the least drop in your dopamine, or to search and search for just the right scene for maximum climax. Also, you may be masturbating in a hunched-over position – or watching your smartphone in bed nightly.

Each of these cues, or triggers, can now light up your reward circuit with the promise of sex ... that isn't sex. Nevertheless, nerve cells may solidify these associations with sexual arousal by sprouting new branches to strengthen connections. The more you use porn the stronger the nerve connections can become, with the result that you may ultimately *need* to be a voyeur, *need* to click to new material, *need* to climax to porn to get to sleep, or *need* to search for the perfect ending just to get the job done.

A prime evolutionary task of adolescence is learning all about sex – both consciously and unconsciously. To accomplish this, the highly malleable adolescent brain wires to sexual cues in the environment.[81] Novel, startling, arousing stimuli can rock an adolescent's world in a way it won't an adult brain, and this showed up in the brain scans of young porn users in a 2014 Cambridge study.[82] This neurochemical reality primes young brains. They learn to define sex according to whatever stimuli offer the biggest sexual buzz.

Adolescents wire together experiences and arousal much

faster and more easily than young adults will just a few years later.[83] The brain actually shrinks after age 12 as billions of nerve connections are pruned and reorganized (as pictured).[84] The use-it-or-lose-it principle governs which nerve connections survive.

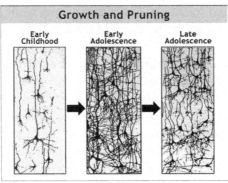

Once new connections form, teen brains hold tightly to these associations. In fact, research shows that our most powerful and lasting memories arise from adolescence – along with our worst habits.[85]

Before 24/7 streaming porn, the usual sexual cues were other teens, or an occasional centrefold, or maybe an R-rated movie. The result was pretty predictable: Peers were a turn-on. Now, however:

I'm 25, but I've had high-speed internet access and started streaming porn videos since age 12. My sexual experience is very limited and the few times I've had sex have been total disappointments: no erection. Been trying to quit for 5 months now and finally have. I realize that I've been conditioned to the point where my sexual urges are deeply linked to a computer screen. Women don't turn me on unless they are made 2-D and behind my glass monitor.

Especially in an overactive adolescent brain, such unconscious wiring can lead to unexpected shifts in sexual tastes. Once again, as psychiatrist Norman Doidge explained in *The Brain That Changes Itself,* 'Because plasticity is competitive, the brain maps for new, exciting images increased at the expense of what had previously attracted them'.

If the majority of a teen's masturbation sessions are porn-fuelled, then brain maps related to Jessica in algebra may be crowded out. Spending years before your first kiss hunched over a screen with 10 tabs open, mastering the dubious skills of learning to masturbate with your left hand and hunting for sex acts your dad never heard of, does not prepare you for fumbling your way to first base, let alone satisfying lovemaking.

In a 2014 article, Norman Doidge wrote, 'We are in the midst of a revolution in sexual and romantic tastes unlike any in history, a social experiment being performed on children and teenagers ... The level of porn exposure is quite new. Will these influences and tastes turn out to be superficial? Or will the new porn scenarios deeply embed themselves because the teen years are still a formative period.'

Fortunately, brain plasticity also works the other way. I see many young guys quit porn and, months later, realise that the fetishes they thought were indelible had faded away. Eventually, they can't believe they once got off to X (and perhaps *only* to X).

Adolescent sexual conditioning likely also accounts for the fact that young men with porn-induced erectile dysfunction need months longer to recover normal sexual function than older men do. This might be because the older men did not start out wiring their sexual response to screens, and still possess well developed 'real partner' brain pathways, or brain maps. Typically they had reliable erections with partners for years before they met high-speed tube sites.

Addiction

A second adaptation that may arise from excessive porn consumption is *addiction*. Interestingly, research on rats recently showed that methamphetamine and cocaine hijack the *same reward-centre nerve cells* that evolved for sexual conditioning.[86] A second study by some of the same researchers found that sex with ejaculation shrinks (for a week at least) the cells that pump dopamine throughout the reward circuit. These same dopamine-producing nerve cells shrink with heroin addiction.[87]

Put simply, addictive drugs like meth and heroin are compelling because they hijack the precise mechanisms that evolved to make sex compelling.[88] Other pleasures also activate the reward centre, but their associated nerve cells don't overlap as completely with sex. Therefore they feel different and less compelling. We all know the difference between munching on chips and an orgasm.

Just as drugs can activate the 'sex' nerve cells and trigger a buzz without actual sex, so can internet porn. Pleasures like golf, sunsets and laughing cannot. For that matter, neither can good old rock & roll. Just because something is pleasurable doesn't mean it's addictive. Sexual arousal is nature's number-one priority and raises dopamine the highest of all natural rewards.

Researchers know that in all addictions, despite their differences, chronic dopamine elevation tips specific neurochemical dominoes, which bring about an established set of core brain changes.[89] These, in turn, show up as recognized signs, symptoms and behaviours, such as those listed in this standard addiction assessment test known as the 'Three Cs'[90]:

1. **craving** and preoccupation with obtaining, engaging in or recovering from the use of the substance or behaviour;

2. loss of **control** in using the substance or engaging in the behaviour with increasing frequency or duration, larger amounts or intensity, or in increasing the risk in use and behaviour to obtain the desired effect; and

3. negative **consequences** in physical, social, occupational, financial and psychological domains.

How great is the risk of porn addiction? Well, it's common knowledge that dopamine-raising substances, such as alcohol or cocaine, can create addictions. Yet only about 10-15% of humans or rats that use addictive drugs (except nicotine) ever become addicts. Does this mean the rest of us are safe from addiction? When it comes to substance abuse, perhaps *yes*.

Yet when it comes to unrestricted access to super-stimulating versions of natural rewards, such as junk food,[91] the answer is *no*,[92] although certainly not every consumer gets hooked.

The reason that highly stimulating versions of food[93] and sexual arousal can hook us – even if we're not otherwise susceptible to addiction – is that our reward circuitry evolved to drive us toward food[94] and sex, not drugs or alcohol. Today's high fat[95]/sugar foods[96] have hooked far more people into destructive patterns of behaviour than have illegal drugs. 70% of American adults are overweight, 37% obese.[97]

We don't know how many people are being negatively affected by internet pornography, given the privacy that surrounds its use, and the fact that users don't necessarily connect porn use with their symptoms. However, a 2014 poll of 1,000 US adults found that 33% of men 18-30 either think that they are addicted to porn or are unsure. In sharp contrast, only 5% of men 50-68 think they are, or might be, addicted.[98]

These supernormal versions of natural rewards have the ability to override our brain's satiation mechanisms – the 'I'm done' feeling.[99] It's hardly surprising that unlimited erotic novelty is compelling for large swathes of the population, including many who would not be susceptible to substance addiction.

I do occasionally drink but not too much. I have no addictions except porn. I grew up thinking it was a normal thing and that everyone does it. I thought that it might even be good for me.

*

I battled with porn addiction for years, whereas quitting smoking was a single decision and I never looked back. Unlike smoking, porn addiction is tied to an underlying biological need, which merges with the addiction and makes everything more difficult.

Are We *Really* Talking About Addiction Here?

Some psychologists and clinicians outside the addiction-neuroscience field claim it is a mistake to employ addiction science to understand behaviours like compulsive gambling and out of control consumption of internet pornography. They argue that addiction only makes sense when talking about substances like heroin, alcohol or nicotine. This view often finds its way into the media. But the latest research into the nature of addiction contradicts this. You may not be aware of it but addiction is perhaps the most extensively studied mental disorder. Unlike most disorders in psychiatry's bible, the *Diagnostic and Statistical Manual* (*DSM-5*), addiction can be reproduced at will in laboratory animals. Researchers then study the causal mechanisms and resulting brain changes right down to the molecular level.

For example, they have discovered that same molecular switch (protein DeltaFosB) initiates key addiction-related brain changes (and thus behaviours) in both chemical and behavioural addictions.[100] These kinds of discoveries are the reason that addiction experts have no doubt that both behavioural and substance addictions are fundamentally one disorder.

Already, some ninety brain studies on internet addicts reveal the presence of the same core brain changes seen in substance addicts.[101] If internet use itself is potentially addictive, then obviously internet porn use is too. Indeed, in a study entitled, "Predicting compulsive Internet use: it's all about sex!" Dutch researchers found that online erotica has the highest addictive potential of all online applications (with online gaming second).[102] This makes perfect sense because addictive drugs only cause addiction because they magnify or inhibit brain mechanisms *already in place for natural rewards*, such as sexual arousal.[103]

In other words, existing internet-addiction brain studies (many of which include internet porn use[104]) already indirectly establish the addictiveness of internet porn as a matter of hard science.

As yet, only three studies (published in 2014) have isolated and analysed the brains of internet porn users. The first of these looked at users who were not addicts: "Brain Structure and Functional Connectivity Associated With Pornography Consumption: The Brain on Porn". It was published in the prestigious *JAMA Psychiatry* journal.[105] In this study, experts at Germany's Max Planck Institute found:

1. Higher hours per week/more years of porn viewing correlated with a reduction in grey matter in sections of the reward circuitry (striatum) involved in motivation and decision-making. Reduced grey matter in this reward-related region means fewer nerve connections. Fewer nerve connections here translates into sluggish reward activity, or a numbed pleasure response, often called *desensitisation* (more on that below). The researchers interpreted this as an indication of the effects of longer-term porn exposure.

2. The nerve connections between the reward circuit and prefrontal cortex worsened with increased porn watching. As the study stated, 'Dysfunction of this circuitry has been related to inappropriate behavioural choices, such as drug seeking, regardless of the potential negative outcome.' In short, this is evidence of an association between porn use and impaired impulse control.

3. The more porn used, the less reward activation when sexual images were flashed on the screen, possible evidence of desensitisation. Lead author Simone Kühn explained, 'We assume that subjects with a high porn consumption need increasing stimulation to receive the same amount of reward. That would fit perfectly the hypothesis that their reward systems need growing stimulation.'[106]

To sum up: More porn use correlated with less grey matter and reduced reward activity (in the dorsal striatum) when viewing sexual images. More porn use also correlated with weakened connections to the seat of our willpower, the frontal cortex.

Keep in mind that this study did not examine causation, but rather correlation. The researchers analysed the brain scans of 64 porn users in relation to a 'pure dosage effect of porn hours'. None were addicts. The scientists also carefully screened potential subjects to exclude people with other medical and neurological disorders as well as substance use.

However, the researchers didn't take the next step of having subjects remove porn use for months to see if the changes reversed themselves. Nevertheless, extensive related research (some of which has recorded improvements after quitting[107]) supports the hypothesis that chronic overstimulation is indeed the culprit.

A forthcoming series of studies by Cambridge University addiction neuroscience experts isolated actual internet porn *addicts* and examined their brains. The two studies published so far confirm that porn addicts' brains respond like those of drug addicts.[108] [109] Said one of the researchers:

> *There are clear differences in brain activity between patients who have compulsive sexual behaviour and healthy volunteers. These differences mirror those of drug addicts'* [110] *... I think [ours is] a study that can help people understand that this is a real pathology, this is a real disorder, so people will not dismiss compulsive sexual behaviour as something moralistic. ... This is not different from how pathologic gambling and substance addiction were viewed several years ago.* [111]

The Cambridge team discovered that, in addicts, the reward centre (nucleus accumbens) showed hyper-reactivity to porn cues (hardcore video clips). This is evidence of *sensitisation,* explained more fully below, which powers cravings in addicts. Incidentally, women porn users also recorded increased cue-reactivity (as compared with controls) in a recent German study.[112]

In contrast, when the Max Planck team (above) looked at *non*-addicted porn users' brains they found less activation of *another* region of the reward circuit. This is evidence of *desensitisation,* or a numbed responsiveness.

In analysing the Max Planck results, the Cambridge team hypothesised that the brain responses to porn might differ between non-addicts and addicts. True. Yet might the visual stimuli used in the two studies go far in explaining the differences? The Max Planck researchers saw decreased responsiveness to half-second exposure to still porn images, which may strike today's porn viewer as ordinary, while the 9-second video clips the Cambridge team used would arouse most porn viewers, addicted or not. In short, perhaps the video clips were proper *cues* for today's users of streaming HD hardcore porn while brief stills were a closer representation of everyday erotic visuals, which had grown duller.

In any case, both hyper-reactivity to addiction cues (hardcore video) and reduced sexual responsiveness to tamer sexual visuals are not surprising in porn overconsumers. *Both increased cue-reactivity and a reduced pleasure response are often seen in addicts of all kinds.*[113]

Readers interested in addiction science and its relevance to internet porn users may want to have a look at this peer-reviewed journal article: "Pornography addiction – a supranormal stimulus considered in the context of neuroplasticity".[114]

No doubt more brain studies on porn addicts are on the way, but already addiction specialists maintain that all *addiction is one condition.* It doesn't matter whether it entails sexual behaviour, gambling, alcohol, nicotine, heroin or crystal meth – many of which addiction neuroscientists have studied for decades. Hundreds of brain studies on behavioural and substance addiction confirm that all addictions modify the same fundamental brain mechanisms[115] and produce a recognized set of anatomical and chemical alterations.[116] (More on these in a moment.)

In 2011 the American Society of Addiction Medicine (doctors and researchers) confirmed the addiction-is-one-condition model by publishing an all-encompassing new definition of addiction.[117] This is from the related FAQs:

QUESTION: This new definition of addiction refers to addiction involving gambling, food, and sexual behaviours. Does ASAM really believe that food and sex are addicting?

ANSWER: The new ASAM definition makes a departure from equating addiction with just substance dependence, by describing how addiction is also related to behaviours that are rewarding. ... This definition says that addiction is about functioning and brain circuitry and

> *how the structure and function of the brains of persons*
> *with addiction differ from the structure and function of*
> *the brains of persons who do not have addiction. ... Food*
> *and sexual behaviours and gambling behaviours can*
> *be associated with the 'pathological pursuit of rewards'*
> *described in this new definition of addiction.*

Even the psychiatry profession's heavily criticised and obsolete bible, the *DSM-5,* has grudgingly begun to recognize the existence of behavioural addictions.[118] Charles O'Brien, MD, chair of the *DSM-5* Work Group on Substance-Related and Addictive Disorders said:[119]

> *The idea of a non-substance-related addiction may be*
> *new to some people, but those of us who are studying the*
> *mechanisms of addiction find strong evidence from animal*
> *and human research that addiction is a disorder of the*
> *brain reward system, and it doesn't matter whether the*
> *system is repeatedly activated by gambling or alcohol or*
> *another substance.*

Outside the addiction field, you can still find vocal addiction naysayers who insist that gambling addiction and porn addiction are not addictions but rather *compulsions.* This is a red herring. I have asked these naysayers, 'how do the neural correlates for a compulsion to use something differ from the neural correlates for an addiction to something?' (*Neural correlates* refer to the brain circuits, neurochemicals, receptors and genes underlying a disorder.)

The 'compulsion' advocates never answer because, in fact, there is no physical difference at the brain level between a gambling addiction and a compulsion to gamble. There is only one reward centre and one reward circuit. Core brain changes seen in behavioural addictions occur equally with drug addictions – and compulsions to use. These are the brain changes associated with addictive behaviour. (Of course, specific addictions each have unique characteristics as well. For example, heroin addiction drastically reduces opioid receptors, which produces particularly severe withdrawal symptoms.)

Here are some brain changes that show up in all addictions, whether substance or behavioural:

1. Desensitisation, *or a numbed response to pleasure.* Reduced dopamine signalling[120] and other changes[121] leave the addict less sensitive to everyday pleasures and 'hungry' for dopamine-raising activities and substances.[122] The addict may neglect other interests and activities that were once high priorities.

Desensitisation is probably the first addiction-related brain change porn users notice. They need greater and greater stimulation to achieve the same buzz ('tolerance'). They may spend more time online, prolonging sessions through edging, watching when not masturbating, or searching for the perfect video to end with. But desensitisation can also take the form of escalating to new genres, sometimes harder and stranger, or even disturbing. Remember: shock, surprise and anxiety can jack up dopamine.

2. Sensitisation, *or an unconscious super-memory of pleasure that, when activated, triggers powerful cravings.* Rewired nerve connections cause the reward circuit to buzz[123] in response to addiction-related cues or thoughts[124] – the 'fire together wire together' principle. This Pavlovian memory makes the addiction more compelling than other activities in the addict's life.

Cues, such as turning on the computer, seeing a pop-up, or being alone, trigger intense cravings for porn. Are you suddenly much hornier (true libido) when your wife goes shopping? Unlikely. But perhaps you feel as if you are on autopilot, or someone else is controlling your brain. Some describe a sensitised porn response as 'entering a tunnel that has only one escape: porn'. Maybe you feel a rush, rapid heartbeat, even trembling, and all you can think about is logging onto your favourite tube site. These are examples of sensitised addiction pathways activating your reward circuit, screaming, 'Do it now!'

3. Hypofrontality, *or reduced brain activity in the prefrontal regions, which weakens willpower in the face of strong subconscious cravings.* Alterations[125] in the prefrontal regions' grey matter[126] and white matter[127] correlate with reduced impulse control[128] and the weakened ability to foresee consequences.[129] A recent German review of brain and psychological studies concluded that reduced brain function in internet addicts may be related to their loss of control over their internet use.[130]

Hypofrontality shows up as the feeling that two parts of your brain are engaged in a tug-of-war. The sensitised addiction pathways are screaming 'Yes!' while your 'higher brain' is saying, 'No, not again!' While the executive-control portions of your brain are in a weakened condition the addiction pathways usually win.

4. **Dysfunctional stress circuits,**[131] *which can make even minor stress lead to cravings and relapse because they activate powerful sensitised pathways.*

To sum up, if these neuroplastic changes could speak, *desensitisation* would be moaning, 'I can't get no satisfaction'. At the same time, *sensitisation* would be poking you in the ribs saying, 'hey, I've got just what you need', which happens to be the very thing that caused the desensitisation. *Hypofrontality* would be shrugging and sighing, 'bad idea, but I can't stop you'. *Dysfunctional stress circuits* would be screaming, 'I NEED something NOW to take the edge off!'

These phenomena are at the core of all addictions. One recovering porn addict summed them up: 'I will never get enough of what doesn't satisfy me and it never, ever satisfies me'. Recovery reverses these changes. Slowly, the addict relearns how to 'want' normally.

Withdrawal Many people believe that addiction always entails both tolerance (a need for more stimulation to get the same effect, caused by desensitisation) and brutal withdrawal symptoms. In fact, neither is a prerequisite for addiction – although today's porn users often report both. What all addiction assessment tests share is, 'continued use despite negative consequences'. That is the most reliable evidence of addiction.

This book has already offered many accounts by porn users who sought more extreme porn as their brains grew less sensitive to pleasure (tolerance). What about withdrawal symptoms? First, as stated, a person can be addicted without experiencing severe withdrawal symptoms. For example, cigarette and cocaine addicts can be thoroughly hooked but will typically experience mild withdrawal symptoms compared with alcoholics or heroin addicts.[132]

However, in the forums I monitor ex-porn users regularly report withdrawal symptoms that are reminiscent of drug withdrawals: insomnia, anxiety, irritability, mood swings, headaches, restlessness, fatigue, poor concentration, depression, social paralysis and cravings. Some also report more startling symptoms, such as shaking, flu-like symptoms, muscle cramps, recurring bouts of depression or anxiety that continue for months, or the mysterious sudden loss of libido that guys call the flatline (apparently unique to porn withdrawal).

> *December and January were tough, and I mean tough! I had serious depression...absolutely no libido at all. Distressing thoughts would run through my brain all day and night and I found myself crying like a baby. My poor little man was a permanently flaccid, useless addition to my body that simply didn't want or fancy real female attention.*

Internet-porn withdrawal symptoms haven't been studied in isolation, but in 2013 Swansea and Milan universities reported that internet addicts suffer a form of cold turkey when they stop using the web, just like people coming off drugs.[133] Most of the addicts studied were accessing porn or gambling.[134]

Not everyone who stops using pornography will suffer withdrawal symptoms, but some do:

> *My symptoms after quitting: extreme exhaustion, restless sleep, muscle aches, joint pains and fever, mild disorientation, tension in the chest/tight breathing and anxiousness.*

> *

> *My withdrawal symptoms are restless legs. My legs won't stay still when I'm sitting in my chair. Disrupted sleep. I'm having trouble sleeping, or I wake up in the middle of the night with my heart beating fast and can't get back to sleep. Headaches. I have a sore throat and feel generally run down.*

To repeat, internet porn withdrawal symptoms sometimes resemble drug withdrawal symptoms because all addictions share specific neurochemical and cellular changes (as well as producing additional, unique changes). Withdrawal initiates a cascade of neurochemical alterations, although brains experience them somewhat differently.[135]

Overriding Normal Satisfaction

Excess consumption of food or sex signals the brain that you have hit the evolutionary jackpot.[136] This kind of powerful neurochemical incentive to grab more is an advantage in situations where survival is furthered by overriding normal satisfaction.[137] Think of wolves, which need to stow away up to twenty pounds of a single kill at one go. Or mating season,[138] when there was a harem to impregnate. In the past, such opportunities were rare and passed quickly.

Now, however, the internet offers endless 'mating opportunities', which a primitive part of the brain perceives as valuable because they are so arousing. As any good mammal would, viewers attempt to spread their genes far and wide, but there's no end to a porn viewer's mating season. He can keep going indefinitely by pumping up his dopamine via anticipation as he surfs: viewing novelty, material that violates his expectations, and driving for sexual arousal – the natural reward that releases the highest surges of dopamine.

Click, click, click, masturbate, click, click, click, masturbate, click, click, click. Sessions can last for hours, day in and day out, sometimes kicking the viewer's evolved 'binge mechanism' into overdrive. Evolution has not prepared the brain for this kind of nonstop stimulation. Experts Riemersma and Sytsma warn that today's porn may cause 'rapid onset' addiction in some chronic users.[139]

How the Brain Keeps Us Bingeing

You already know that dopamine sets off the neurochemical events that cause addiction-related brain changes[140]. But the actual molecular switch that initiates many of the lasting brain changes is the protein DeltaFosB.[141] Dopamine surges trigger DeltaFosB's production. It then accumulates slowly in the reward circuitry in proportion to the amount of dopamine released when we chronically indulge in natural rewards[142] (sex,[143] sugar,[144] high fat, [145] aerobic exercise[146]) or virtually any drug of abuse. DeltaFosB takes a month or two to dissipate, but the changes it causes can remain.

Why am I telling you about DeltaFosB? Unlikely as it may seem, this single neurobiological discovery dismantles the claim that porn addiction does not exist. DeltaFosB accumulating in the reward centre of the brain is now considered to be a sustained molecular switch for both behavioural and chemical addictions.

What does DeltaFosB *do* as it accumulates? It turns on a very specific set of genes that physically and chemically alter the reward centre.[147] Think of dopamine as the foreman on a construction site barking the orders and DeltaFosB as the construction workers who actually pour the cement.

Dopamine is yelling, 'This activity is really, really important, and you should do it again and again.' DeltaFosB's job, as the construction worker, is to have you *remember and repeat* the activity. It does this by rewiring your brain to want 'it', 'it' being whatever you have been bingeing on. A spiral can ensue in which wanting leads to doing, doing triggers more surges of dopamine, dopamine causes DeltaFosB to accumulate – and the urge to repeat the behaviour gets stronger with each loop. When you think, 'Nerve cells that fire together wire together', think DeltaFosB.

Wiring together everything associated with porn use to hammer your reward circuitry via specially constructed pathways so that you crave porn is known as *sensitisation*. All of the brain changes initiated by DeltaFosB tend to keep us overconsuming or, in the case of internet porn, riveted to what the brain perceives as a Fertilization Fest.

This set of neurochemical dominoes certainly did not evolve to create addicts. It evolved to urge animals to 'Get it while the getting is good.' But the point is that the mechanism of elevated dopamine leading to DeltaFosB accumulation is the same mechanism that initiates *both* sexual conditioning *and* addiction. Both start with a Pavlovian super-memory of pleasure (sensitization), which then triggers powerful 'do it again!' urges. Porn users would be naive to imagine that they are impervious to this biological process.

The obvious question is: 'How much is too much?' The answer is simple: 'whatever amount of stimulation causes the accumulation of DeltaFosB and corresponding addiction-related brain changes.' That will differ for each viewer, so questions such as 'does this visual count as porn?' or 'how much porn use will cause addiction?' are misguided. The former is like asking whether it's slot machines or blackjack that causes gambling addiction. The latter is like asking an obese junk-food addict how many minutes she spends eating.

The fact is, the brain's reward centre doesn't know what porn is. It only registers levels of stimulation through dopamine spikes.[148] The mysterious interaction between the individual viewer's brain and the chosen stimuli determines whether or not a viewer slips into addiction.

Interestingly, some people who claim not to be addicted, and who can quit with relative ease, still experience severe sexual dysfunctions related to their porn use[149]: delayed ejaculation, erectile dysfunction, inability to orgasm during sex or loss of attraction to real partners. It's likely that the brain changes associated with sexual conditioning are behind their symptoms.

Dopamine is odd. It shoots up when something is better than expected (violates expectations), but drops when expectations are not met.[150] With sex, it's nearly impossible to match internet porn's level of surprise, variety and novelty. Thus, once a young man thoroughly conditions himself to porn, sex may not meet his unconscious expectations. Unmet expectations produce a *drop* in dopamine – and erections. (A steady stream of dopamine surges is imperative for sustaining sexual arousal and erections.)

Adolescents are especially vulnerable here because their reward circuitry is in overdrive.[151] In response to internet novelty it produces higher spikes of dopamine. It is also more sensitive to dopamine[152] and their brains produce more DeltaFosB[153] (to 'remember and repeat'). As a consequence, the teen brain can deeply condition itself to internet porn with surprising ease, such that real sex truly feels like an alien experience to some. Learning pleasurable sex then requires months longer than it does for men who grew up without the internet and conditioned themselves to actual partners first. The latter are simply re-learning.

The adolescent brain's over-sensitivity to reward also means its owner is more vulnerable to addiction.[154] And if that's not scary enough, remember that a natural sculpting process narrows a teen's choices by adulthood.[155] His brain prunes his neural circuitry to leave him with well-honed responses to life.[156] By his twenties, he may not exactly be *stuck* with the sexual conditioning he falls into during adolescence, but it can be like a deep rut in his brain – less easy to ignore or reconfigure.

Isolating Cause and Effect

Addiction naysayers generally insist that porn users who develop problems all had pre-existing conditions, such as depression, childhood trauma or OCD. They insist that excessive porn use is the *result*, not the cause, of their problems. Of course, some porn users do have pre-existing issues and will need additional support.

However, no one falls into addiction without engaging in chronic overstimulation. Moreover, the implication that young people without pre-existing conditions can engage in excess without risk of developing symptoms is not supported by research.[157] For example, in a rare longitudinal study (tracking young internet users over time) researchers found that 'young people who are initially free of mental health problems but use the Internet pathologically' develop depression at 2.5 times the rate of those who don't engage in such use.[158] (Researchers had also adjusted for potential confounding factors.)

A year later, a fascinating experiment, which would be impossible to duplicate in the West, began when Chinese researchers measured the mental health of incoming students.[159] A subset of these students had never spent time on the internet before arriving at university. Twelve months later, scientists evaluated the internet newbies' mental health again. Fifty-nine of them had already developed internet addiction. Said the researchers:

After their addiction, significantly higher scores were observed for dimensions on depression, anxiety, hostility, interpersonal sensitivity, and psychoticism, suggesting that these were outcomes of Internet addiction disorder.

The researchers compared the before and after scores on mental health in the newbie addicts and found that internet addiction seemed to have *caused* significant changes in their mental health. From the study:

– Before they were addicted to the Internet, the scores of depression, anxiety, and hostility for students with Internet addiction were lower than the norm.

– *After their addiction* (**one year later**), *the dimensions … increased significantly, suggesting that* depression, anxiety, and hostility *were outcomes of* Internet addiction, *and not precursors for* Internet addiction. (emphasis added)

Said the researchers:

We cannot find a solid pathological predictor for Internet addiction disorder. Internet addiction disorder may bring some pathological problems to the addicts.

This study suggests that the students' internet habits caused their psychological symptoms. More recently, Taiwanese researchers showed that there is a correlation between teen suicide ideation/attempt and internet addiction, even after controlling for depression, self-esteem, family support, and demographics.[160]

In another study, Chinese researchers confirmed that while high-risk internet abusers exhibit definite signs of depression (such as loss of interest, aggressive behaviour, depressive mood, and guilt feelings), they show little evidence of a permanent depressive trait.[161] In other words, their symptoms apparently stem from their internet abuse, not underlying, pre-existing characteristics.

Just recently, Chinese researchers measured depression, hostility, social anxiety and internet addiction in 2,293 7th graders twice, a year apart.[161] Those who had become addicts exhibited increased depression and hostility compared with the non-addicted group. Further, those who began as addicts but were no longer addicted at the end of the year showed decreased depression, hostility, and social anxiety compared with those who remained addicted.

Even more recently, Belgian researchers assessed 14-year old boys' academic performance at two points in time. They found that 'an increased use of Internet pornography decreased boys' academic performance six months later.'[163]

These findings are consistent with the results informally reported by thousands of recovery forum members who quit porn and experience benefits in mood, motivation, academic performance, social anxiety, etc. Their severe symptoms, followed by noticeable improvements, undermine the assertion that internet problems arise only in people with pre-existing disorders or characteristics.

More on Porn-Induced Sexual Dysfunctions

Research reveals that erections require adequate dopamine in the reward circuit[164] *and* the male sexual centres of the brain.[165] Not long ago, Italian researchers scanned the brains of guys with 'psychogenic ED' (as opposed to 'organic ED', which arises from issues below the belt). Their scans revealed atrophy of the grey matter in the brain's reward centre (nucleus accumbens) and the sexual centres of the hypothalamus.[166] Loss of grey matter equates with loss of nerve cell branches and connections with other nerve cells. Here, this translates into reduced dopamine signalling (reduced arousal). It's like your 8-cylinder engine is now sputtering along on only 3 cylinders.

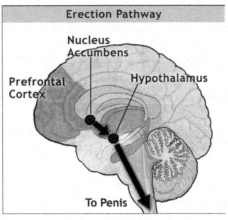

The study is evidence that psychogenic ED is *not* always caused by an individual's state of mind at a particular moment. It can be a consequence of changes to the reward circuitry that result in persistently reduced dopamine signalling. This could help explain porn-induced sexual dysfunctions, such as erectile dysfunction, delayed ejaculation and inability to climax at all during intercourse – and why such symptoms generally require weeks or months to reverse.

The Italian finding is consistent with findings in the new German study on porn users published in *JAMA Psychiatry*.[167] Both studies show less grey matter in the reward circuitry. In the German study, subjects who used the most porn had less grey matter and showed less arousal to sexy pictures. To answer the age-old question, size does matter, at least when it comes to grey matter.

As mentioned earlier, guys who started out on high-speed internet porn typically need months longer to recover their sexual health than guys forty and older. Loss of grey matter in the reward circuitry (desensitisation) appears to play a role in porn-induced erectile dysfunction, but the fact that young guys often need longer to recover points to deep sexual conditioning during adolescence. Desensitisation and other brain changes arising from chronic overconsumption can be picked up in brain scans, but sexual conditioning doesn't show up in pictures of the brain. Confirmation of this effect must come through self-reports of symptoms and recoveries.

As we saw earlier, adolescence is a key developmental window during which mammalian brains are primed to adapt their mating behaviour to arousing cues in the environment. Thereafter, brains begin to prune away unused circuitry – perhaps the very circuitry related to the pursuit of real partners that these guys' adolescent ancestors would have developed and strengthened as a matter of course.[168] Here's a typical account of a younger guy who had thoroughly wired his sexuality to internet porn:

> *What you're likely wondering is, 'For the love of god does the ED get better or am I torturing myself for no reason?!' I wondered that too. The answer is 'Kind of,' then 'Yes!' What you're likely going to experience once you do engage in sex is your brain saying, 'what the hell?' It is not used to actual sex as its primary way of being sexual. Real contact begins the 'rewiring' process. You will be re-sensitizing yourself to actual sex. Sex after rebooting and rewiring feels WAY BETTER. Can't even describe it in words. So there will be a rewiring process where you may sputter and have a few backfires but eventually you fire on all cylinders. These days? Zero ED, I don't even have to think about it.*

Are Some Porn Users Misdiagnosed?

Although symptoms such as erectile dysfunction, social anxiety, concentration problems and depression are quite different, they share a common finding in the scientific literature. As I explained, one brain change that occurs with addiction is desensitisation. Again, this term refers to a general dialling down of a person's responsiveness to all pleasure – a baseline drop in dopamine and reduced dopamine sensitivity. And it's worth repeating that the German researchers discussed in the previous section found evidence of desensitisation even in *moderate* porn users.

In the case of porn use, desensitisation could potentially account for lots of symptoms heavy users report. A decline in dopamine signalling is associated with all of these:

– Diminished sexual behaviour,[168] which, as noted, is a possible cause of sluggish erections/climaxes,
– Decreased risk-taking[170] and increased anxiety, combined with a tendency toward angry overreaction,[171] any of which can decrease willingness to socialize,
– Inability to focus,[172] which can account for concentration and memory problems, and
– Lack of motivation[173] and healthy anticipation, which can lead to apathy,[174] procrastination, and even play a role in depression.[175]

In fact, when a medical student courageously allowed doctors to deplete his dopamine briefly using a pharmaceutical,[176] look what happened:

> *During increasing dopamine depletion in this case, a range of subjective experiences appeared and disappeared consecutively. These experiences resembled negative symptoms [loss of motivation, dulled senses, decreased fluency, lower mood, fatigue, poor concentration, anxiety, restlessness, feelings of shame, fear], obsessive-compulsive symptoms, thought disorders, and anxiety and depressive symptoms.* [Bracketed items are listed elsewhere in the article cited.]

Addiction researchers have measured a decline in dopamine

and dopamine sensitivity in the brains of addicts of all kinds, including internet addicts.[177] We also know that this decline can happen very quickly with 'natural rewards' such as junk food.[178] [179]

The flipside is that when dopamine and related neurochemicals are properly regulated, sexual attraction, socializing, concentration, sexual responsiveness, and feelings of wellbeing are more effortless. I suspect that a return to normal dopamine signalling helps explain why many guys report similar sets of diverse improvements after they unhook from excessive consumption of internet porn.

Researchers are just beginning to isolate the symptoms caused by frequent pornography consumption. For example, Swedish researchers recently tracked 16-year olds for two years. Frequent use of pornography at baseline predicted persistent headaches, feeling stressed and insomnia at follow-up.[180] Unfortunately, many healthcare providers still assume that internet porn use cannot cause symptoms like these, or depression, brain fog, low motivation or anxiety. As a consequence, they inadvertently misdiagnose internet porn users as having primary disorders without inquiring about their internet habits. Porn users are then surprised when quitting porn resolves their other symptoms:

> *I don't think society knows what internet porn really does to a man. All they really associate porn with is ED. Porn turns a man into a scared boy. I was socially awkward, depressed, had no motivation, couldn't focus, very insecure, weak muscle tone, my voice was weaker, and I had absolutely no control over my life. Men are going to the doctors getting prescribed all kind of meds, when really it often comes down to porn and what it does to your brain and body. I'm off porn now and feel better than I felt in years.*

*

[Day 91, after two years of striving to quit porn] As someone who has struggled with diagnosed depression since my teens (YES, I see an undeniable connection to porn and fapping), I can say that I am starting to experience a better self-image, have been processing life troubles much better. I don't let stress make me hostile or hopeless like before. In other words, I'm a lot less depressed.

*

As a man with genetic depression, being porn-free has done more for me than any drugs I have ever had to take. It is as if this makes me more alert, attentive, and happier than Wellbutrin, Zoloft or the other drugs I was cycled through.

*

Quitting is the anti-depressant I needed. 9 months ago I was a 25-year old university drop out, working a job I hated and depressed. A few months after I quit porn, I got my superpowers. I did a lot of things for the first time, including kissing a girl within two minutes of meeting her and being invited to another girl's apartment. I think that I don't have depression anymore. There still are downhills, but nothing like before with no energy for anything and suicidal thoughts. My secret? In the last month I've used internet for maybe an hour. I have decided to start university once more in September even though I have to pay for everything myself.

A thorough understanding of how the brain adapts in response to chronic overstimulation becomes vital when people seek help for porn-induced problems. Professionals educated prior to high-speed porn were sometimes trained that sexual tastes are somehow as innate as sexual orientation. Instead of encouraging patients to experiment with reversing their porn-induced tastes, they may propose more drastic treatment:

In 2012, I tried to get help from a professional psychotherapist/ sexologist. I plucked up the courage to tell the therapist that I also had a 20-year problem with compulsive porn use. I hit a wall of incomprehension. This psychotherapist tried to convince me that it was a high sexual desire (hypersexual disorder) and irreversible paraphilias (anal sex and rough porn scenes). The therapist said porn addiction doesn't exist and wanted to prescribe me a potent anti-androgen drug to reduce sex drive. I didn't agree, being aware of its side effects, like gynecomastia [breast growth].

Evidently, healthcare providers are also treating some young men for erectile dysfunction and delayed ejaculation who simply need to quit porn. In a single day, I read two posts to this effect. The first young man's uncle was a psychiatrist, who had told him porn-induced erectile dysfunction was impossible. The young man experimented anyway and recovered. The other guy was a 32-year old man whose doctor finally recommended a penile implant when injections didn't work (let alone Viagra). He resisted, discovered the information on how porn can cause ED, experimented and recovered. Another man faced a similar situation:

The medical profession is far behind the times. I spent thousands of dollars on doctors, including a well known urologist specializing in ED (had to travel hours for that one); thousands on tests; thousands on pills. 'Erection to porn means it's in your head ... take some Viagra.' Not once did any health care professional say to me, 'Hey, watching porn too much can cause sexual dysfunction.' Instead, they offered other explanations, which are not proven to be linked to ED and typically did not apply to me anyway (e.g. anxiety, stress...even though you don't show any indication of either; diet...even though your weight is normal and you eat a balanced diet; low testosterone...even though low T hasn't been linked to ED except in extreme cases, and your T is not really low).

Then there's absolutely horrible advice from 'sexologists' who are so bent on being 'sex positive', they not only deny the potential negative consequences of porn use, they actively ridicule the notion of porn-induced ED.[181] So, though I feel stupid for not making the link between porn and ED myself, the fact is I sought professional advice and porn was never brought up except in a positive light: 'Everyone does it, it's normal...in fact, it's healthy.' I evaluated the possibility of surgical intervention. It would be between $25k and $30k out of pocket and the results are not encouraging (penile revascularization). The day after that appointment I stumbled on this information. Oh my god...what a revelation and relief.

And it works. I'm not 100%, but I've improved dramatically and things keep getting better. All I had to do was quit fapping to porn. Unreal. Honestly, I'm a bit angry given that I sought solutions from professionals, including specialists, who graciously accepted my hard earned cash yet gave me bad advice.

How many men are getting outdated information and treatments they don't require? Do their brains primarily need a chance to return to normal, and therefore to pleasure and sexual responsiveness? For some, recovery from porn-induced problems appears to be a natural outcome of giving up chronic overstimulation.

Bottom line, given what we know about the links between behaviour and brain function, it seems reckless to prescribe psychotropic drugs to young people without first addressing potential overuse of today's porn.

3

Regaining Control

The road of excess leads to the palace of wisdom.
William Blake

Although people report many benefits from recovery, the biggest gift is regaining control of your life. A recovered porn user explains:

Despite what some people say, quitting will not make you into a god of confidence and ability, although for the first few months it'll really feel like that. Quitting will give you more control of your own life. It's a little bit like the transition from adolescence to adulthood. Instead of acting on impulse, you'll be learning self-restraint and mindfulness with one of your most primal instincts, which will flow over into every part of your life and make your life's decisions be entirely up to you.

When I started this 500 days ago, I had trouble concentrating; I couldn't commit to a goal for more than a week at a time. Whenever I had a day off I wasted it in lazy indulgence, knowing that I could be doing more with my time. Now, I can handle 50, 60 hour work weeks regularly without even noticing it. Now, I can exercise regularly and stick to it. Now, I'm in a relationship unlike any I've ever been in because I can finally treat my partner as another human being rather than sometimes as an object of desire (I now know firsthand that my own desires aren't as important as they make themselves out to be). Now, I'm constantly improving myself instead of just wishing I could.

The first step toward regaining control is to give your brain a rest from all *artificial sexual stimulation* for several months. Shift your attention to real life. Among other things, this will help you establish whether chronic overconsumption of pornography, or some other issue, is underlying your symptoms. Ideally, an extended time-out also allows you to:

– restore the sensitivity of your brain's reward circuitry so you can again enjoy everyday pleasures,

– reduce the intensity of the 'gotta have it!' brain pathways that drive you to use,

– re-establish your willpower (strengthen the brain's frontal lobes), and

– reduce the impact of stress such that it doesn't set off severe cravings.

Next, you stay consistent because it can take many months, or even a couple of years, for the 'I want to watch porn right now!' pathways to fire less frequently – and then die down.

Some people call this process 'rebooting'. It's a way of rediscovering what you are like without porn in your life. The idea is that by avoiding artificial sexual stimulation you are shutting down and restarting the brain, restoring it to its original factory settings, even.

The metaphor isn't perfect. You cannot go back in time to a 'restore point', or erase all the data, as you would when you wipe clean a computer's hard drive. However, many people do reverse their porn-related problems by giving the brain a well deserved rest from porn, porn fantasy and porn substitutes. And often the metaphor is a useful part of the process. After all, the problematic behaviours and symptoms of porn addiction are material in nature. They are inscribed in the structures of the brain. By changing behaviour we change those structures. Over time new ways of life are reflected in changes in brain function.

Through trial and error, rebooters have discovered that 'artificial sexual stimulation' refers to more than internet porn. Surfing Facebook, YouTube, or dating or erotic services sites for images is like an alcoholic switching to lite beer: counterproductive. In short, artificial sexual stimulation includes anything your brain might use in the way it has been using porn: cam2cam erotic encounters, sexting, reading erotica, friendfinder apps, fantasizing about porn scenarios ... you get the idea.

The goal now is to seek your pleasure from interacting with real people without a screen between you, and awaken your appetite for life and love. At first, your brain may not perceive real people as particularly stimulating in comparison with the novelty-at-a-click furnished by internet porn. However, as you consistently refuse to activate the porn pathways in your brain, your priorities gradually shift. Rebooters make all kinds of interesting discoveries:

I actually went a full 6 months without even visiting a porn site. When I next saw one I was surprised by how cheesy and corny porn looked. Since then I really haven't had much interest in watching it. Porn is to sex what looking at a photograph of a Ferrari is to driving one.

*

When I got back from a conference yesterday I was exhausted physically and mentally. But this time I discovered an inner reservoir of energy I never expected to find. The sex was incredible, passionate, and unbelievable. I felt like I was 20 years old all over again. After 5 years of being 'too tired' to have sex in times like these I now know the problem isn't about fading chemistry with my wife but about wasting my sexual energy fapping to porn all the time.

Initially the rebooting process is challenging. Your brain

is counting on you to supply the artificially intense 'fix' of dopamine (and other neurochemicals) it has adapted to through porn use. It can get very testy when its fix is not forthcoming when it summons you with a craving. However, freedom lies in allowing it to return to normal sensitivity and weaken any addiction pathways. Only then will you be truly free to set your own priorities without loud neurochemical signals stressing you and overriding your choices.

One guy described the process this way:

When you remove a source of pleasure from the brain, it is like taking away the leg of a table. The whole thing becomes rocky and unstable. The brain has two options: one, to make you hurt like hell in every way it can think of to 'encourage' you to put the table leg back again, or two, to accept that the table leg is really gone, and figure out how to re-balance without it. Of course, it tries Option One first. Then, after a while, it gets to work on Option Two, all while still pushing Option One. Eventually, it seems like the brain re-balances, giving up on Option One, and fully succeeding at Option Two.

In this chapter we'll start with standard tips that rebooters frequently share with each other. Then we'll look at the most common rebooting challenges and pitfalls. Finally, we'll address a few questions that often come up.

Keep in mind that brains, histories and circumstances vary. There is no magic bullet that works well for everyone. Pick and choose the tips that might serve you in retraining your brain. Do not get caught up in, 'am I doing this right?' It is you who decides the length and parameters of your reboot, depending on your goals and current situation. Many rebooters (without porn-induced ED) aim for 100 days or three months, broken up into shorter interim goals. Those with ED sometimes need far longer.

A reboot is your laboratory. If your plan isn't producing the results you want, adjust. Recognize that it often takes a couple of months to know if any particular approach is working, so unless you have fallen back into bingeing on pornography, stay your chosen course for a couple of months at least.

> *It's amazing what you learn doing this. I think I now fully understand the saying that 'knowledge is power.' Once you know how something works and how it affects you, it's much easier to muster the willpower to make a change if you wish.*

Word to the wise: Rebooting doesn't guarantee that a person who has had porn problems can safely return to internet porn in the future. Many guys learn this the hard way. They assume their recovered erections mean they can use porn or porn substitutes, only to end up with ED again. Deeply etched porn pathways can easily spring back to life.

Recommended Suggestions

Here are some of the most familiar tips I see on the recovery forums:

Managing access

Remove all porn

Delete all porn from your devices. It can be a wrench, but this action sends your brain the signal that your intention to change is ironclad. Remember to delete back-ups and the trash. Also get rid of all bookmarks to porn sites as well as your browser history.

One guy claimed to have 'heirloom porn' that he absolutely could not part with. He burned it to a disk, wrapped it, duct-taped the packet like it contained the proprietary formula for Coca-Cola, and stored it in an inconvenient, out of sight location. Once he recovered he chucked it away.

Move your furniture around

Environmental cues associated with use can be powerful triggers because they themselves release dopamine. This fires up anticipation and activates sensitised addiction pathways. Drug addicts are told to avoid friends, neighbourhoods and activities associated with previous use.

You can't avoid yourself or move, but you can make some changes, and then take care not to use porn in the new configuration. For example, consider using your online devices only in a less private location, which you don't associate with porn use. Or transform your 'porn space' environment. Get rid of your 'masturbation chair' or simply move your furniture around, as this guy did:

> *The reorientation of my apartment has been wonderful as I don't feel any of the same associations that I did in the past set-up. It's weird how moving everything a few feet and turning items a few degrees can change the energy surrounding your attachment.*

More ideas:

> *I put my desktop computer away. It's the one I've masturbated on for years, and it's the one that's least reliable with the filtering. I don't use it for anything but porn and wasting time. I can finish all I need to get done on my laptop.*

> *

> *I converted my desk into a standing desk, which has worked miracles on my poor internet browsing habits. Since I'm not comfortably sitting in a chair my computer usage has been reduced to things I need to do instead of whatever I want.*

Consider a porn blocker and an ad blocker

Porn blockers are not fail-proof. They are like speed-bumps.

They give you time to realize that you're about to do what you really don't want to do. Early in the process of recovery, before the self-control mechanisms in your brain are restored to full working order, blockers can be quite helpful. Eventually, you won't need them.

Free porn blockers are available at these sites:

– Qustodio - http://www.qustodio.com/index2

– K-9 – http://www1.k9webprotection.com

– Esafely.com – http://www.esafely.com/home.php

– OpenDNS – http://www.opendns.com/home-internet-security/parental-controls/

I highly recommend OpenDNS or some other kind of web filtering service, especially if it comes with a 3-minute delay before new settings take effect. That way, even if you falter, the 3 minutes give you enough time to realize you really don't want to do this, and unset those settings. Block all sexual categories, all dating categories and all blog categories. Tumblr is a really sneaky one you can't afford to let loose.

Note: If you are a videogamer, using a porn-blocker can be risky. Your brain is accustomed to getting some of its dopamine hits from finding ways around obstacles. You may unthinkingly treat the porn blocker like just another videogame quest. If this happens, delete your porn blocker and try extinction training (below) or some other approach.

In any case, consider using an ad blocker. That way you won't have to see wiggling images in your sidebar when making holiday plans or ordering vitamins. Many guys find ad blockers extremely helpful in warding off temptation. 'AdblockPlus' is free.

Consider a day-counter

Various forums offer free day-counters. Beneath each post you make a bar graph appears showing your progress to your goal, and it updates itself automatically. Some people, particularly men, find it very satisfying to track their progress visually.

Counters get mixed reviews. The risk is that if someone slips back into porn use, he may think of his days as game points, and use his newly reduced day count to rationalise continuing to use porn for a while 'because I won't lose many accumulated days.' Such binges erode progress more than isolated incidents do, so if you get a day-counter, take a long-term view. Be pleased with your overall count of porn-free days, without rationalizing about short-term 'scores' or thinking it's safe to return to porn once your goal is met.

Ultimately, what matters is not days but brain balance. Brains do not all return to balance on a set schedule, and while brains definitely need time to reboot, accumulated days aren't the whole story. Brain balance also benefits from exercise, socializing, time in nature, increased self-control, better self-care and so forth.

An alternative to setting a long day-count goal is to set mini-goals for yourself. That way you repeatedly get a rewarding sense of achievement even as you crawl toward a longer goal.

Extinction training (not for everyone)

Remember Pavlov's dogs? You may not realize it, but Pavlov didn't just teach his dog to salivate at the sound of a bell. He later taught it to *stop* salivating to the bell by ringing the bell and then withholding meat (repeatedly).

This process is known as 'cue extinction'. You weaken the link or pathway between a stimulus and a habitual response. Some porn users are able to use this same principle to strengthen their self-control:

(Age 16) Every time I was on my PC I would open a porn website. Once the site opened I would turn it off so I could test how much willpower I had. Those first 2 weeks were the hardest by far and I still don't know how I was able to do it. After 30 days clean I could tell I was forgetting about porn. Today I've been clean for 90 days and I barely think about porn. I feel like a new person. During this 3 months I masturbated a few times (like 5), but I never watched porn. Getting off is just something that every teenager needs to do now and then.

If extinction training (sometimes known as Exposure Response Prevention Therapy) is too risky for you because glimpses of porn sites throw you into a binge, try an indirect approach to strengthening your willpower first. Exercise (or any beneficial stressor) and meditation are good choices. Both are discussed below.

Support

Join a forum, get an accountability partner
Involvement in an online community where others are experimenting with giving up porn is helpful for most people. It can inspire you, give you a place to rant, supply the good feelings that come from supporting others, and generate new tips for speeding your progress. Said one guy:

Don't fight this fight alone. In the end, you'll be the one pushing yourself to success, but an online community can give you that little bit of extra motivation when you're at your absolute lowest.

Sites such as NoFap.org and Reboot Nation facilitate finding accountability partners. This is a way for you and one of your peers to support each other in more depth while still preserving your anonymity. One-on-one support definitely speeds some people's progress.

The downside of both accountability partners and forum participation is that they are online activities. As problematic internet porn use is an internet-based issue, you need to spend less time online, not more. While most people agree that a forum helped them during the first phase of recovery, eventually some find that a recovery forum can itself become a way to avoid real life. At that point, some choose to check a forum only when they need encouragement.

Addiction has a social context, as does recovery. Whether you find support and recognition online or off is less important than that you find it.

Therapy, support groups, healthcare
A good therapist who understands that behavioural addictions are as real as any other addictions can be very helpful. Some of them facilitate support groups for people struggling to quit internet porn. There are also self-run 12-Step groups, both online and off.

If you are struggling with additional issues, such as childhood trauma, sexual abuse or family problems, which naturally make emotional attachment challenging, a good counsellor can be a sound investment.

Again, if you think you may have obsessive-compulsive disorder (OCD), you may need medication for a bit when you attempt to quit pornography to ease the anxiety of withdrawal. See a doctor. An OCD sufferer said:

> *The antidepressants have really helped. They kick me in the rear and force me to look at my situation positively and not get so wound up in it all.*

Keep a journal
Support yourself by keeping a record of your progress.

Rebooting is not a linear process. There are good days and bad days, and on the bad days your brain will try to persuade you that you have made no progress and there is no hope that you ever will. Often by reading earlier entries from your journal you can swiftly put things back in perspective:

> *When the cravings were bad, I would look at my journal and see how I'd come too far to quit. Put a password on it if you don't want someone else to find it.*

Journals also allow you to get things off your chest that you would not feel comfortable sharing with anyone else. Alternatively, you can share those things in an anonymous online journal. Various forums allow you to journal for free (NoFap.org, RebootNation.org, YourBrainRebalanced.com). The added advantage of an online journal is that you and your peers can offer each other support and advice based on journal entries.

Managing Stress, Improving Self-control and Self-care

Exercise, beneficial stressors

Of all the techniques rebooters experiment with, exercise seems to be the most universally beneficial. It's an excellent distraction from urges, also improves self-confidence and fitness, and is even associated with better erectile function in men under 40.[182]

Exercise is a solid mood regulator. Scientists surmise that it can help ease addiction because acute bouts of exercise increase dopamine concentrations, and regular exercise leads to sustained increases in dopamine and related adjustments.[183] This helps counteract the chronically low dopamine signalling that haunts recovering addicts before their brains reboot.[184] Here are comments from two people:

I cannot overemphasize the importance of push-ups. They are always accessible, and take only thirty seconds or so to do a good 20. They will get your heart pumping, and will divert your body's attention away from those urges almost instantly. If urges still linger, do sets with a few seconds break, until your arms feel like they'll fall off. Then you'll be in the clear.

*

Lift weights. It helps. If you're feeling self-conscious use the machines instead of free weights. The staff at the gym will help you if you have no idea how to use the machines.

Exercise is known as a 'beneficial stressor'. That is, by stressing your system slightly it causes it to respond with enhanced feelings of wellbeing. Some rebooters report that beneficial-stressors, in general, can be very helpful in resetting the brain's sensitivity to pleasure. Visit www.gettingstronger.org for articles and research about the physiology behind exercise, intermittent fasting, daily cold showers, and so forth.

The latter were once laughed off as a mainstay of Victorian theorists of manliness, but daily cold showers get rave reviews from many who seek a quick route to restoring lost willpower and increasing emotional equilibrium. Cold showers have even been proposed as a potential medical treatment for depression.[185]

I'm on an 81-day streak right now, taking the coldest showers I can. My desire to escape is strong, but I resist, and walk out of the shower like I'm the king of the world.

Remember, it's about finding what works for you. If a cold shower improves your mood, and makes you less tempted to waste time slumped in front of a computer, then it is useful, especially when your body is struggling with withdrawal.

It's not a good idea to overdo anything, but you knew that already.

Get outside
Researchers have found that time in nature is good for the brain. It boosts creativity, insight and problem solving.[186] Rebooters have noticed this too:

> *There's something very, very powerful about being away from technology and in a natural environment that accelerates rewiring in my experience.*

> *

> *I go out each morning before sunrise, jog to a hill, climb up it, sit and watch the sunrise, and thank the Earth and creation for my existence. It feels like a big cuddle, so there you go...*

If you live in a city, walk to parks. According to researchers at the University of Sheffield, tranquil, living environments can positively affect human brain function.[187]

> *Get outside into the natural light and breathe fresh air. We weren't meant to look at glowing rectangles and breathe recycled air 24/7*

Socializing
Humans evolved as tribal, pair-bonding primates. Our brains cannot easily regulate mood on their own, at least not for long. It's not unusual to feel anxious or depressed (or self-medicate with an addiction) when isolated.

By the same token, connection is some of the best health insurance the planet offers. It helps reduce the hormone cortisol, which can otherwise weaken the immune system under stress. 'It's much less wear and tear on us if we have someone there to help regulate us,' explained psychologist/neuroscientist James A. Coan in the *New York Times*.[188]

When recovering users force their attention away from their habitual 'relief', their reward circuitry looks around for other sources of pleasure. Eventually it finds the natural rewards it evolved to find: friendly interaction, real mates, time in nature, exercise, accomplishment, creativity, and so forth. All ease cravings.

Connection and companionship don't have to be verbal to be soothing. If you've been feeling anti-social, start simply. Here are comments from three recovering users:

> *There are a lot of places where you can get used to being out and around people that are pretty nonthreatening. Hang out and read in a library or bookstore, or take a magazine to a coffee shop or park bench. Or take long walks outside. Making this a habit helps get me out of my own head and makes me feel more like of a member of society.*

*

> *I just smile every time I feel awkward, haha. And it works.*

*

> *I am building new platonic relationships with people I have met at networking events, clubs, and so forth. I have been doing some volunteer counselling work once a week, and try to do at least one 'random act of kindness' each day for a complete stranger. This definitely helps bring a bit of balance.*

Another easy option is to attend meetings that have a set structure, such as Toastmasters.

Whatever you choose, practice eye-contact with those you pass. Start with older people. Make a game of it. See if you can improve your score each time. Once you're comfortable, add a smile, nod or verbal greeting until your natural charisma kicks in automatically.

Meditation, relaxation techniques
Daily meditation can be very soothing for anyone struggling with the stress of withdrawal. Research also shows that daily meditation helps the rational part of the brain, called the frontal lobes, to stay in the driver's seat.[189] Meditation thus strengthens what addiction has weakened, even as it quiets the primitive parts of the brain that drive impulsive behaviour.

Forum members' thoughts on meditation:

I heard that you should not think about quitting your addiction. Instead you should learn how to meditate. The more you meditate the stronger your mind becomes and the weaker your addiction gets. So I have increased my meditation time. My thoughts about porn have reduced drastically.

✳

When I meditate consistently, the part of my brain that knows that I have to leave porn behind (the pre-frontal cortex) has much more influence. And when I don't meditate regularly, the part of my mind that comes up with rationalizations to use porn as way to deal with boredom and stress has more sway. It seems that the battle to overcome porn is literally a battle between the rational, planning functions and the more emotional, reactive parts of the brain. Meditation is probably the best tool for putting the pre-frontal cortex in the driver's seat.

Creative pursuits, hobbies, life purpose
The first few weeks are primarily a battle of distraction. Put all your extra time, energy and confidence to use on other efforts that keep you preoccupied. A rebooter explained the

importance of filling your time differently by exploring and learning new things:

> *You can't expect to live the exact same lifestyle you've been living, (i.e., get up, do a little work, surf web, do a little more work, surf web, surf NSFW, do a little work, surf web, etc.) and expect anything to change. That pattern won't magically disappear without conscious effort.*

Your brain will thank you. And, just like learning new things, creativity is both a great distraction and inherently rewarding because of the anticipation of achieving something important to you:

> *I enjoy music, and quitting has helped both my creative ability for music, as well as my enjoyment of listening to it. I've probably 'composed' about 20 songs in my head in the last few months since quitting. Also, I've found I'm much more creative with my jokes and conversational threads. All of a sudden conversations feel like playing music. It is both enjoyable and impressive, actually. I am planning to join the Improv club at university, and see where I can take this. Stage-performance doesn't seem daunting at all, anymore. Exciting, if anything.*

> *

> *I'm a writer and musician, though I have let my art fall by the wayside over the past few years as I retreated farther and farther into porn. I thought that I was dealing with writer's block because I could not allow myself to put words on paper or notes on strings. Since I started this journey, however, I have recommitted myself to my art and am now working on three songs with a fourth starting to work its way out of me.*

Many people report taking up hobbies, new and old, as they reboot. Here are comments of three guys:

I've taken up cooking and baking. It's a great distraction, it's fun, and I get a reward when I'm finished.

*

Yoga gets me out of the house and helps me burn off some steam. Lots of beautiful women there too. Very beautiful women. Mmm...women.

*

I started playing my guitar again, going to the gym, learning how to eat more nutritiously, and how to dress more stylishly.

Tip: Limit activities that cause 'empty' dopamine highs, such as frequent, intense videogaming, junk food, gambling, trolling Facebook, Tumblr, Twitter and Yahoo, meaningless TV, and so forth. Instead, steer for activities that produce more lasting, sustainable satisfaction even if they aren't as rewarding in the short-run: having a good conversation, organizing your work space, receiving/giving a therapeutic massage, goal-setting, visiting someone, building something or gardening. In short, anything that gives you a sense of connection or moves you toward longer-term objectives.

A powerful distraction like internet porn can be a form of self-medication for boredom, frustration, stress or loneliness. But if you're reading this book you probably realize that chronic use of a supernormally stimulating distraction is a Faustian bargain. Eventually, it can take a toll on your goals and wellbeing.

The better you feel, the less you need to self-medicate. Getting fit and learning to eat healthily are a start. For thousands of years humans had to wrestle with the challenge of maintaining brain balance without today's drugs. Many left insightful, inspiring solutions that are now available to all via the internet. There's no need to reinvent the wheel. Dig around. Think big. Take the time to develop a philosophy of life. Act on it.

Attitude, Education and Inspiration

Be gentle with yourself
Those who reboot with relative ease keep a sense of humour, accept their humanness, love sex but respect their sexuality, and gradually steer themselves into a new groove. They don't bludgeon themselves, or threaten themselves with doom.

Sex is a fundamental drive, and giving up the intense stimulation of regular porn use is a big shift for your brain. It's best to ease your way through the transition, forgive yourself if you slip, and keep going until you get where you want to be. Think of snowboarding or surfboarding. Stay flexible.

Learn more about what's going on in your brain
Whether rebooters know a lot or a little about science, they generally value learning how the brain interacts with a supernormal stimulus such as today's internet porn. It explains how they got where they are and how to change course:

> *Just knowing what is going on in the brain and what is causing it gives me a feeling of relief. It's crazy how slyly the mind can trick you. With this new knowledge I feel that I can recognize what is happening and act on it before it's too late. I highly recommend watching some of the videos on http://yourbrainonporn.com.*

www.yourbrainonporn.com, the site I created, is a clearing house for relevant science about the brain. Resources range from easy-to-understand articles and videos by lay people to vast collections of medical abstracts and studies about behavioural addiction.

Keep yourself inspired
Rebooting can be a mighty challenge, and it helps to find a well of inspiration to draw from on a regular, even daily, basis. Maybe you frequent an online forum where there is lots of encouragement. Maybe you have a favourite philosopher or spiritual book you find soothing and uplifting:

> *The second thing that really helped me was reading. My favourite was a book that said to take a goal you want to accomplish; decide what steps you have to take in order to accomplish that goal; and do it no matter how you feel. I decided to have a better social life, so I joined university clubs when I didn't feel like it. I joined some academic clubs for my major when I didn't feel like it. I started conversations with people in my classes when I didn't feel like it. I went to parties that I knew about when I didn't feel like it. I went to bars and clubs with people when they invited me when I didn't feel like it. I asked girls on dates when I was really nervous about it. It was really hard, but eventually I got a really great group of friends.*

There are hundreds of inspiring recovery self-reports, culled from various forums, on www.yourbrainonporn.com. Click on 'Rebooting Accounts' under 'Rebooting Basics'.

Rebooting Challenges

Withdrawal
Perhaps because our culture does not yet appreciate the honest-to-goodness physical addictiveness of today's pornography, the severity of withdrawal symptoms can catch those who quit by

surprise. The discomfort can easily derail a reboot, as this guy warns:

> *Withdrawals suck. We don't talk enough about them. They are why we fail. They are our brain's reward centre begging us, threatening us, punishing us, pleading with us, rationalizing with us why we need to use porn. Withdrawals are painful, they are physical, mental, and emotional pain. They are the jitters, the shakes, the sweats, odd pains in odd places, the brain fog we feel when quitting, and our brain's way of telling us all that unpleasantness can go away with just a little harmless fix. When going through withdrawal I felt I had a sinus infection and my teeth actually hurt. I did not have a sinus infection and my teeth were fine, but my brain, at some level, had to make me feel bad to try and make me feel good through a porn release.*

In all addictions, terminating chronic overstimulation of the brain prompts very real neurochemical events.[190] [191] [192] Typically, these include an exaggerated stress response and a powerful sense that the world is hopelessly grey and meaningless in the absence of the missing stimulus. The first two weeks are often the toughest:

> *Let me tell you the truth right when you decide to take the challenge: You won't be able to do it. Or, at least, that's what you're going to think every single day, and it'll feel so true that you just can't take it anymore. You will be going through the emotional ups and downs and downs of withdrawal. You are like a man setting out to climb a tall mountain who has never walked before. At first it will seem impossible, but as you walk a little bit more each day, your muscles, i.e., your willpower, will grow and it will become possible. So take it one day at a time, always. Don't look at what you're doing as fighting a war to quit for X days, or it*

seems too big to take on. Realize that what you're doing is just saying 'no' once. When that urge comes up, you say 'no', you scream into a pillow, you scream internally, you throw those thoughts away, you distract yourself, you realise how much better you've done without porn, and how much you have to lose going back and starting over and maybe not even getting this far. You don't let that urge go anywhere. You say 'no', that one time, and you do that every one time that it comes up. That's it. Not X days of constant willpower, just a subtle lifestyle change, a quiet 'no' whenever the random desire flickers up and tries to take hold.

As explained, our brains evolved to strive for neurochemical balance. If we chronically bombard them with intense stimulation, they mute neural signals by reducing sensitivity to neurochemicals like dopamine. Chronic overstimulation can thus lead to a zombie-like numbness to pleasure and emotion. Daily life can seem dull and pointless.

Yet when we remove the exaggerated stimulation, numbness gradually reverses itself. Mood swings are often the first sign that something is shifting:

My brain is like a see-saw right now. My day can turn from a great one to a near suicidal one in the space of a few hours. It's difficult to endure but it reassures me that something is trying to correct itself.

Gradually, colours return, enthusiasm increases and stability reigns. In his TEDx talk: "The Pleasure Trap", psychologist Doug Lisle gives examples of how overeaters can reverse food cravings with periods of fasting or juice-only. The same principle of increasing sensitivity by removing overstimulation applies to all natural rewards, including masturbation to internet porn.

Some porn users report little withdrawal distress. Others

report severe withdrawal symptoms. Here's a 26-year old, long-time porn user's report:

> *The first week I had the worst type of insomnia imaginable. I don't remember falling asleep at all the first 6 days. In my mind, it made Hell Week of Navy SEAL training look easy. During the weeks that followed, things started turning around a bit but really became noticeable after about 3 months. I actually started getting energy to do things.*

Some people had no reason to suspect withdrawal would be so agonizing:

> *Not having had a major porn problem, I assumed the benefits would be marginal. But if you think you don't have an addiction, try stopping and see what happens. In my case, a period of quite punishing withdrawal symptoms. They lasted for at least a month. Something was clearly profoundly affecting me neurochemically, as within a 24hr period I might experience the extremes of a kind of shimmering, exultant euphoria followed by a moribund depressive blackness. Around the month mark I started feeling significantly better about myself and things began falling into place effortlessly; people seemed better disposed towards me, my body language improved, I started joking around at work more and generally seeing the lighter side of life.*

Common withdrawal symptoms include: irritability, anxiety or even panic, unaccustomed tears, restlessness, lethargy, headaches, brain fog, depression, mood swings, desire to isolate, muscle tightness, insomnia, and severe cravings to use porn.

Emotional things come up heavily: depression, strange anxieties, worthlessness. It was everything that I had been struggling with – all at once. It was like having a really bad day x 10! And, of course, the horniness. You really start to learn to control your fantasies because if you don't, you'll feel the discomfort.

Less common, but not unusual, symptoms include: frequent urination, shakes, nausea, tension in the chest creating difficulty breathing, despair, hot flashes or feeling cold even in front of a fire, overeating or loss of appetite, unaccustomed wet dreams, semen leakage when using the toilet, and fullness, pressure or aching in the testicles (cold water helps).

Mood swings like a pregnant 13-year old girl. I'll see a neat-looking tree and then cry about it. Intense, insatiable desire for human contact...yet a terrible fear of actually getting it. Insatiable food cravings...Almost ate an entire cake in 24 hours. I have a VERY SHORT FUSE, you idiot! LOL I treat people like crap when I feel like this. This is the worst symptom.

Another frustrating thing about withdrawal symptoms is that recovery isn't linear; it's up and down. Some people only experience acute withdrawal symptoms during the first two or three weeks. Others still have sporadic withdrawal symptoms for months, informally dubbed 'Post-Acute Withdrawal Syndrome', or PAWS.

Just wanted to give some hope to those of you struggling with the mental ailments associated with this shit. For well over a year and a half, I haven't been able to find joy in much of anything. Now, I'm beginning to feel music the way I used to. I can enjoy a conversation with a stranger instead of struggling through the social anxiety associated with it.

> *Simply put, as much hell these past couple years have put*
> *me through, I am truly improving. There's no doubt about*
> *it. This is SO clearly PAWS, or post-acute withdrawal*
> *syndrome. Absolutely no doubt. The "up and down" nature*
> *of the symptoms, the slowwwwww nature of the recovery,*
> *and the symptoms themselves.*

Good days gradually become more frequent, but bad days continue for a long while before the brain is really back to normal. It's unwise to measure your progress against any particular individual's recovery time. Some people simply need longer than others to restore brain balance.

Flatline

One young man described the flatline as 'the gruelling, mysterious initiation one endures but never speaks of.' It's a standard withdrawal symptom in guys with porn-induced erectile dysfunction, but it also happens to some who don't have ED at the time they quit. I touched on this temporary effect earlier, but there's more to say. Here's a typical description of the flatline:

> *After a few days of brain tantrums (cravings), I went into*
> *a flatline for weeks. Basically I felt totally indifferent about*
> *girls, sex, everything. A little voice from the porn beast*
> *nagged at me in the back of my mind, but mostly, I just*
> *didn't care. And my penis was very lifeless and small. It was*
> *like somebody just pulled the plug on whatever machine*
> *provides my sex drive. No libido at all.*

Needless to say, some guys bail out of recovery at this point and rush back to porn, afraid that they will permanently lose it if they don't use it. About six years ago, however, a courageous 26-year old Australian kept going – and discovered that somewhere around week seven, his flatline ended and his libido (and erections) came roaring back.[193] Since then, many guys have braved the flatline and documented their recoveries.

No one yet knows what causes the flatline, but here's one guy's theory:

We started masturbating to internet porn very young, kept doing it like crazy until we exhausted our minds and bodies. When you become exhausted, your brain and body enters sleep mode (that we call flatline) in order to recover so it can react to stimulation again. If we had let it rest back then it would probably been a flatline of only a few days before things returned to normal. But we didn't let it rest. Despite being in a flatline, we used porn to continue until we reached rock bottom. So now it doesn't take a few days for things to recover. It takes a few months or even longer in some cases. But it passes.

Perhaps the flatline arises from a constellation of normal withdrawal events, combined with stubborn changes in the sexual centres of the brain. I suspect the sexual centres (in the hypothalamus) are implicated because other kinds of addicts don't temporarily lose sexual function when they stop using.

Certainly everyone's flatline is somewhat unique in terms of severity and duration. Some guys' libido and erections come back together, either gradually or all at once. For other guys, libido returns before erections. And some report that erections return before libido. Whatever its origins, the flatline is definitely weird. Prior to high-speed porn, cutting out porn use was *not* associated with a severe, temporary drop in libido.

If you're having porn-related sexual performance problems, should you tell your partner? Many guys report that it really helps to educate a partner about the flatline and its causes. Here's a 23-year old woman whose boyfriend of the same age needed 130 days to return to normal:

Tell your girlfriend. It takes the pressure off you and helps you to avoid hurting her. PIED [porn-induced ED] *is nothing to feel bad about. Nowadays porn is really common and nearly every guy is using porn or has used porn sometime (and I believe every girl knows that). It could happen to anyone, as you don't have to be an excessive porn user to get your brain messed up. My boyfriend really tried to explain everything and I'm so thankful for that! It feels so much better to know what's going on. It also brings you closer together when your partner includes you in something like that because then it becomes a thing you get through together.*

Not every guy who quits porn experiences a temporary loss of libido (flatline) during recovery. However, the percentage of those who report flatlines appears to be rising as the guys who started on high-speed comprise a growing portion of ED sufferers. As one guy said,

Some guys flatline a long time, some don't, some never get one. It's difficult to gauge anything because this problem is so new. Hopefully in a couple years we'll start to see some trends and be able to give better advice to those who have just quit. Unfortunately we're the pioneers in this.

Insomnia

It's important to stay well rested as fatigue can trigger porn use. However, many rebooters have relied on their porn ritual as a sleep-aid for years. Without it, sleep is elusive at first. (Insomnia is also a common withdrawal symptom.) Find what works for you, and keep in mind that the problem will fade with time.

I thought fapping was the only way I could sleep, but only 10 days in I'm already sleeping great. Falling asleep when my head hits the pillow is truly awesome.

Avoid replacing porn use with alcohol. Yes, it will help you fall asleep, but alcohol can wake you up too early, not fully rested. It's also not a good idea to replace an addiction with something else that is potentially addictive. Here are some suggestions that have worked for others:

The first week was pretty rough for me in terms of sleep quality. One thing I did to break out of it was not to use my laptop/read in bed. I set it up on the kitchen table and would only lie down in bed when I got tired.

*

Definitely get a reading lamp. Something about having just that one light on in the room shining on your book will make you ve-he-heh-ry sleepy.

*

I started running late at night. When I get back I take a shower and hit the sack. It puts me to sleep instantly.

*

I turn on music I enjoy that my mind can focus on. Puts me to sleep almost every time.

*

Reading works well for me if I can't sleep. It's a 'replacement behaviour' for masturbating to porn. I've also worked hard at telling myself that missing sleep for a night isn't the end of the world. That really helps.

*

My approach was consistent exercise, as much sunlight as possible (natural melatonin), and abiding by the 'use your bed only for sleep and sex rule' – which for single me translated to 'use your bed only for sleep'.

*

If restlessness gets super bad, I actually do Kegel exercises [pelvic-floor exercises], even in the middle of the night. They tend to ease the longing/withdrawal by redistributing the energy, or whatever. The muscles get a little attention for a while with the kegeling and tend to 'go back to sleep'.

*

Get up earlier. It's also the best time to fit in a workout. You'll be tired by the time it is time to go to sleep in the evening.

*

I usually put something over my eyes and ears like a rolled up t-shirt. It helps me.

*

What works for me is to wake up and go to bed at regular times, and to avoid intense physically activity immediately before sleep.

*

Lie on your back and list everything that you are grateful for. When I first started doing this, my gratitude list was long. Now, I barely get through being thankful for my friends and my dog and I'm dead asleep.

Some guys have benefitted from supplements, herbal teas, such as camomile, and other home remedies:

For insomnia, I drink red date soup or miso soup.

Triggers

One man described triggers as, 'the external factors that make you think about porn.' Common triggers include: TV shows and movies with erotic content, porn flashbacks, morning wood, use of recreational drugs or alcohol, words that remind you of a porn site/actor and suggestive ads. Said one guy:

The only thing that feels worse than relapsing is relapsing because you got too drunk or high to control yourself.

But states of mind can also be triggers: boredom, anxiety, stress, depression, loneliness, rejection, fatigue, frustration, anger, failure, feeling sorry for yourself, desire to reward yourself for an accomplishment, overconfidence, jealousy, and being hungover.

Procrastination also triggers many a relapse. The result has been dubbed 'procrasturbation'. Keep a list of things you want to accomplish as well as a list of risk-free activities for those moments when you just don't have the motivation to do something productive.

Obviously, triggers are somewhat unique to each brain. Here are some less common ones: hot showers, too much sugar or too many carbohydrates, too much caffeine, Russian bride ads, websites like Stumbleupon, YouTube, Imgur and Reddit, stalking old romantic interests on Facebook, being on the computer for a long time without hourly 15-minute breaks, videogames, a full bladder, self-absorption, handling one's genitals, clothing that rubs the genitals, masturbation, smartphone, computer, waiting for code to compile and hunger.

Triggers are both problems and solutions. They can drive you mad during rebooting (at first), but they also show you when to be on high alert. Some rebooters take drastic measures for a bit:

I refused to have an internet connection at home and a smartphone. Both are relatively easy to live without for a month or two while your body resets.

Triggers are what addiction experts call 'cues'. How do they work? Your brain has wired up nerve-cell pathways between your reward circuitry and memories of anything *associated* with porn-arousal. Anything that activates these pathways is a 'cue', or trigger. During evolution, the ability to react to cues worked in your ancestors' favour by helping them not to miss valuable opportunities.

Within your brain these special cue-related pathways cause an abnormally high spike in electrical activity, which induces cravings. This all happens unconsciously. All you know is that you instantly have an overwhelming 'need' to use porn. It can feel like a matter of life and death, such that all your resolutions take flight.

In drug addicts the cue-induced spike can be as high as the spike from actually taking the drug,[194] and this is likely true for heavy porn users as well.

I caught a glimpse of a porn pic the other day and there was a distinct buzz in my brain, almost like a hot flash. Fortunately it freaked me out enough to get away fast.

The bad news is that trigger-pathways sometimes stay around for a long time, even after you are otherwise fully rebooted. They do weaken. For example, an alcoholic who has been sober for 20 years may no longer be triggered by beer commercials. Yet if he drank a beer his sensitized pathways might light up causing him to lose control. Similar things happen to former porn users. They become immune to cues that were formerly risky, but if they use porn again they may binge.

You will need to be mindful of triggers for a long time, especially powerful ones, so it pays to work out what they are and be well aware of them. You also need to have a predetermined response in mind for when you face one. With alertness, expectation and advance preparation, overcoming an urge is do-able. They usually pass if you can distract yourself for about ten minutes.

These men explain how they use triggers to their advantage:

> *One day I am browsing the web when my parents decide to go out. I didn't want to go, so I keep doing my stuff. When they close the door, something clicks in my head. Suddenly, a big desire for porn pops into my mind. I was turned on by the closing of a door! That was the first time I realized that 'the parents leaving home' is another trigger for me. Obvious, but I hadn't noticed it. Now, every time my parents leave the house, I go out for a walk, call a friend or just stop using my computer and do something useful.*

*

> *My biggest problem was always lying in bed with my iPhone. Definitely an easy access trigger. I also used porn almost exclusively at night. What I do now is at 11 pm, I shut down all electronics. I put my laptop in my closet, set my alarm on my phone and put it far away from my bed. Then I go wash my face, brush teeth, etc. I then journal or read until I'm tired. This takes away all triggers and temptations. Instead of leaving my mind to wander I am engrossed in a book.*

When you feel The Urge, ask yourself:

- What emotions I am feeling?
- What time is it?
- Who else is around?
- What did I just do?
- Where am I?
- What could I do instead that would meet my needs?

Could you go for a run, prepare a healthy snack, learn a new word in another language, work on that novel you've been meaning to write or call a friend? Choose a response that furnishes a sense of accomplishment, connection or self-care.

Finally, once you have identified the trigger and decided upon an alternative reward for that situation, record your plan, 'When _____ occurs (trigger), I will _____ (new routine), because it gives me ____ (the reward)'. Rewards might be more energy, something to be proud of, better health, feelings of happiness, the satisfaction of taking care of business, increased confidence, better mood, improved memory, reduced depression, desire to socialise, better erections, and so forth.

If you consistently 'face and replace', your new behaviour will eventually be automatic. If for some reason you can't act on your new routine, do what Olympic athletes do and *visualize* yourself acting on it in minute detail.

Emotions
People who quit porn often remark that they feel more emotions. Why is this a challenge? Because unfamiliar emotions can be overwhelming at first, especially if they are unwelcome. Here are some typical accounts:

> *From unexplainable happiness to crippling sorrow, I now experience emotions like never before. Masturbation to porn had numbed these extremes, leaving me dull and complacent.*

*

> *You will encounter emotions you haven't felt for years, maybe never. Girls that didn't matter to you before will all of a sudden be the centrepiece to your f--king life. That exam you failed? You don't blow it off; you worry about your grade; you worry about the final coming up in two weeks. And this is good; hell it's great. This is the suffering that you learn from, that lets you grow you as a person. But*

it will hurt. At points you'll feel sad, confused maybe even depressed. Don't fall into that trap. Emotions pass, memories fade, and you will come out stronger for it. Remember, you have years of emotional growth and maturity to come into. It might not be easy, you may not feel comfortable, but it is worth it.

As this guy pointed out, you can't have the highs without being willing to face the lows:

Porn, at its core, is much like any other addictive substance or behaviour. It DOES numb your pain, but therein lies the problem. You see, you can't selectively numb an emotion or feeling without numbing every other emotion and feeling. So even though these things dull the sting of vulnerability, loneliness, sadness, disappointment and fear, they also dull the positive range of emotions like happiness, hope, joy and love.

Chaser

The term 'chaser' is often used to describe intense cravings that sometimes follow orgasm. Like withdrawal symptoms, the chaser can derail a reboot in a heartbeat. Two guys describe the chaser:

The chaser effect is counterintuitive but real. I had little urge to fap while my girlfriend was out of the country, but as soon as we started having sex again my urges to use porn became stronger.

*

I sometimes feel hornier in the days following orgasm. At such times, I also have strong feelings of attraction for other women.

Some guys also notice a chaser effect after a wet dream; others don't. In any case, these intense, often unexpected cravings after orgasm can throw an unwary rebooter into a binge:

> *After rebooting I hooked up. We headed to bed. I start tearing clothes off and I'M HARD STRAIGHT AWAY (woohoo!). We have sex for about 2 and a half hours, which HAS to be a record for me. But I experienced the dreaded chaser effect. I was so horny the next morning that I jerked off while she was in the shower. I felt really depressed later that day. In fact, I masturbated quite a few times.*

*

> *After three months porn-free, my new girlfriend and I got each other off, and now, a day or two later, I'm definitely noticing powerful urges to masturbate and look at porn again. It seems so contradictory, but it's happening. I'm masturbating more and I even looked at homemade porn yesterday.*

*

> *I noticed that after bingeing on porn, you really need to push yourself to get back on track because orgasm makes you hornier. The first three days are difficult.*

*

> *I don't have any problems getting laid, but I chose to do my last 30 days or so on hard mode [without partnered sex]. So worth it, and I didn't have to mind the chaser effect, which can be ever so tiresome.*

The chaser is probably an amplified version of the natural neurochemical swings that can follow any climax:

> *After the relapse, the next two days were very difficult. I had extreme difficulty focusing. I could really feel the dopamine withdrawal in my head as my brain felt really*

slow and numb. *My words were slurred and I had difficulty communicating. The urge to masturbate and have sex were a lot stronger than before.*

Happily, sometimes the chaser can help kick-start libido after a long flatline:

The morning of day 68, something very strange happened which I never experienced as a teen: a wet dream. Looking back on this event now from 91 days, I feel like it was the changing point for me, almost like a re-birth. Since then I really started to see the benefits of rebooting. I'm more energised and my ED seems to have cleared up.

People sometimes report that the chaser effect eases over time as the brain continues to finds its balance after rebooting. In fact, the disappearance of extreme chasers can be a sign that the rebooting process is progressing:

Ever since I masturbated Sunday night with my first full blown hard-on using minimal stimulation, no fantasy and surprising endurance to orgasm, I have been feeling a bit more energized and horny. Clear-headed, no real chaser. It's safe to say I am on the upswing.

This husband found a particularly good use for his chaser:

Being that we just made sweet love last night, my wife decided to tip toe down the hall, and see what I was looking at this morning. (She knows about the chaser effect.) So I did as any warrior would do. I showed her exactly what the chaser effect really is! I chased her into the bedroom to demonstrate that I only chase HER now. Left late for work...Worth it!

Disturbing dreams, flashbacks

People often remark that they recall their dreams better after quitting. This can be enjoyable or not:

> *Since I started with nofap, one of the things I have noticed is that my dreams are back. When I was fapping like crazy during the last 10 years, I honestly didn't have one single dream, or only a few.*

Vivid dreams seem to be a normal part of the mental housecleaning process of unhooking. Often people dream they are relapsing as the brain tries to activate familiar brain loops, but eventually such dreams fade.

> *I've been having the most f--ked up dreams, the sort of shit I don't feel comfortable telling anyone about. I understand it's just my mind working its way through withdrawal, but I hope it ends soon. I could really go for a good night's sleep again.*

Porn flashbacks, too, are common during rebooting, and they can cause extreme distress:

> *There are so many times I can't see a stranger or friend for who they are. I just see flashes of them naked, girls or guys. I totally understand that normal people fantasise about someone they really like (a teenager boy who can't pay attention in class because he's thinking of how his teacher looks naked, for instance). So it's not the fact that I'm mentally undressing people that's upsetting. It's the fact that it happens SO OFTEN and in response to such random occurrences, triggers and unwanted triggers. Even when I don't find the person attractive, or I don't want to find them attractive. Such as elderly people or younger children. My mind is just so on the fritz. I can deal with it if I'm just*

passing someone on the street and can quickly snap back and forget about it. But if it's someone I'm actually engaging in a conversation with it almost escalates in a panic attack. I end the conversation quickly and find a quiet place like a bathroom or go on a walk to calm myself down. It sometimes feels as if someone is controlling how I think and I have no say in it. My old porn mind is what's driving it I think.

Best to treat flashbacks like dreams. That is, regard them as mental housecleaning rather than evidence that the reboot isn't working. Just acknowledge them and let them pass without assigning them any meaning. Tune into your senses and shift your attention to what is going on around you. Relax and breathe deeply. Note: Those with OCD tendencies may have a harder time dismissing flashbacks. They assign significance where there is none.

Shame cycle
Many of today's internet porn users grew up with online erotica and are quite blasé about its use. If they feel shame, it's about their inability to control use, not about porn content or use. Their shame evaporates as they regain control.

However, if your porn use is associated in your mind with parental/spousal/religious shaming, threats or punishment – or tangled up with rigid ideas about masturbation – then you may need help reframing your porn use and your self-image. Interestingly, forbidden activities can be unnaturally arousing.

Dopamine rises sharply – especially in teens – when anticipating doing something novel or taking a risk, including doing something forbidden. This neurochemical spur urged our adolescent ancestors to risk embarking for new territories and avoid inbreeding. This makes 'forbidden fruit taste sweetest.' To repeat, research shows that anxiety actually increases arousal.[195]

With all that extra dopamine screaming, 'Yes!' it's easy for the primitive reward circuitry of the brain to *overvalue* condemned activities. They register as hyper-arousing, which means they *also* offer temporary comforting oblivion when feelings of shame strike. This explains how some users fall into a 'shame-binge-shame' cycle.

It would be reckless to claim that the full story is known, as far as the brain chemistry of addiction is concerned. But this biological frame of neuroplasticity – and the computer analogy in the idea of rebooting – gets much closer to the facts of the matter than either conservative angst about sexuality per se or liberal complacency about the innate harmlessness of porn.

Interestingly, people (including religious ones) on the forums we monitor often make rapid progress in rebooting after they re-frame their porn challenge in *biological* terms. They learn how dopamine drives risky behaviours and why chronic overstimulation causes a rebound effect that actually makes cravings and distress worse, thus increasing the 'need' for self-medicating with more porn:

> *I no longer see my addiction as the influence of demons or the natural expression of my wicked sinful heart, but as a very human, very natural (albeit misplaced) desire for sexual intimacy. It was a bad habit, reinforced by neurochemicals, but nothing mysterious or ethereal. I realized that I already had the power to control my actions. And so I did. I realized that the life I wanted to lead was incompatible with porn use, so I made that decision. 'Simply' doesn't mean easily, of course.*
>
> *Success in this area has given me the confidence to tackle other challenges. Since I've started this 90-day streak, I've lost over 20 pounds; I've started swing dancing; I joined a band; and I'm seeing a girl. I'm not talking about superpowers here. All this potential was already inside of me, trapped behind my porn habit. I have more confidence.*

I love myself. I look in the mirror, and I don't feel regret. I think this is how normal people feel. I hate the amount of time I've wasted feeling guilty and ashamed, but I now look forward with a clear conscience. I love my life.

The key seems to be to channel lots of energy into constructive action and self-compassion – and away from excruciating, yet arousing, inner battles.

Common Pitfalls

Edging
What derails more reboots than any other factor? Edging. That is, masturbating up to the edge of orgasm, repeatedly, without climaxing (often while watching something arousing on the internet). This practice is not uncommon on 'nofap' forums where people sometimes persuade themselves that ejaculation is the main problem and internet porn is secondary.

A rebooter explains why edging is unwise:

Instead of achieving orgasm and ending it, you train your brain to be bathing in arousing neurochemicals for hours. It's the worst thing you can do, bar none. The worst. I think most of us weren't addicted to porn, but rather to edging to porn.

In men, edging stresses the prostate. Also, it does not prepare you well for sex with a real person. It's typically tied to prolonged visual stimulation, rapid-fire novelty, clicking from scene to scene, and your own hand (or sex toy).

Dopamine is at its peak when on the verge of orgasm. Therefore edging also keeps dopamine as high as it can naturally go, perhaps for hours. The brain is getting strong signals to strengthen the associations between arousal and whatever the viewer is watching, be it fetish or merely screen. Chronically elevated dopamine also risks causing addiction-related brain changes, such as the decreasing sensitivity to pleasure.

In the pre-internet days, guys would usually masturbate, orgasm and be done with it within a matter of minutes. Orgasm sets off neurochemical changes that inhibit dopamine for a while. That normally spells some relief for sexual frustration. Placing your foot on the dopamine gas, without ever hitting the brake results in a continuous state of cravings without satisfaction:

> *What really got me going down the porn death path was when I changed my habit from doing it* for the orgasm *to doing* it for the sensation leading up to the orgasm.

Be aware that, at first, you may not find a single climax without porn satisfying, just as you may not find masturbation without porn stimulating enough to climax. This is because your brain is not feeling rewards normally. That can work in your favour while your brain is rebalancing itself. More than one recovering user has commented that once he stopped viewing porn, the urge to masturbate eased a lot, because without porn, masturbation was not that interesting. No need to force yourself to climax. Be patient.

Fantasising

Research on mental imagery indicates that fantasising or imagining an experience activates many of the same neural circuits as performing it.[196] In other words, fantasising over hook-up apps or escort ads reinforces your sensitized (addiction-related) pathways, which are looking for their jollies from internet-based novelty.

Most people report that avoiding fantasy early in a reboot is very helpful – including during sex with a partner – because avoidance actually reduces cravings. However, if someone has little sexual experience, it may *eventually* be helpful to engage in realistic fantasy about real potential partners in order to help rewire the brain to real people (instead of screens). After all, humans have been engaging in sexual fantasy for eons.

The key may be to *avoid placing* real people into your favourite porn scenarios. Two guys share their advice:

> *Fantasy is regarded as something risky at first because the first few months our fantasies are nothing but modified versions of the porn scenes. The fact that your brain is somewhat numb to pleasure and creativity means you can't clearly imagine how that hot girl would look naked. Or what loving, caring sex would be like. Solution? 'Let's just recall that porn scene that kept us edging for hours', says your brain. There lies the danger; it's not in the act of fantasising itself. A healthy person who has natural fantasies about someone will not get himself into trouble, while a porn addict who keeps fantasising based on his porn past will only make things worse. My opinion is that once you start to recover, if your mind starts fantasising on its own, without being extreme or unrealistic, you should allow it. Don't necessarily reinforce the fantasy, but allow it to be.*

*

> *If a fantasy even remotely resembles porn, it should be off the table during a reboot. Two reasons:*
>
> *(1) Porn fantasies can lead to relapsing.*
>
> *(2) They can reinforce the screwed up neural circuitry that we're attempting to undo by rebooting. Your brain doesn't make a distinction between imagery that comes from a computer screen or inside your own mind, so running porn-like imagery through your brain is little different from watching porn.*
>
> *Now that said, I don't think that **all** fantasy is bad and*

counterproductive. I've found that during rebooting, pretty much for the first time in my life, I've spontaneously begun to have another type of fantasy that involves intimacy but not sex. These fantasies involve things like exchanging smiles, holding hands, giving back or foot massages. I know that may sound corny, but these fantasies are actually very vivid and enjoyable. I don't think of them as weaker versions of sexual fantasies since they are qualitatively different. I've found this other type of fantasy actually has a positive effect. BTW, I never edge or masturbate during such fantasies (if I did they'd probably become sexual).

Using porn substitutes

This is another easy way to derail your reboot. If you're trying to quit porn, it's easy to rationalize looking at, say, pictures of women in bikinis instead. After all, that's not porn, right? Actually, the primitive part of your brain *doesn't know what porn is.* It simply knows whether something is arousing (to you) or not. (Your brain is in good company. In 1964 Justice Potter Stewart of the US Supreme Court famously claimed that, while he couldn't define pornography, he knew it when he saw it.) So if you find bikini shots hot then they're also problematic.

Opinions as to whether something on your screen constitutes porn are irrelevant. What really matters are spikes of reward-circuit dopamine (and other neurochemicals) associated with artificial sexual stimuli. The question to ask is, 'What type of brain-training led to the problems I'm experiencing, and am I repeating it?'

Would browsing Facebook because you find it arousing activate sensitized addiction pathways and reinforce your addiction? Sure. You are searching, clicking and surfing in pursuit of two-dimensional sexual novelty because your brain is hungry for stimulation. It can slow your recovery. On the other hand, bumping into hard-core images, then immediately closing the page, is actually strengthening your willpower (frontal lobes). Remember, the goal is to reset the brain so it becomes excited by the real deal.

Obviously, the issue isn't 'nakedness'. Which scenario is more like porn addiction?

1. Surfing a dating app while imagining sex with clothed people, as you click from picture to picture, or

2. An afternoon in a nudist colony?

Number one, of course. Internet porn addiction is not an addiction to naked or erotic; it's an addiction to novelty. Screen novelty. One guy summed up what he learned:

> *Why are you browsing YouTube videos of girls dancing in shorts? What's the point of sexting, webcams, phone sex, fantasising constantly, reading erotic stories, browsing dating profiles (without the intention of contacting them), typing pornstar names on Google image search, checking out social media sites, etc?*
>
> *All of these activities increase your urge to masturbate. They reinforce the very same pathways you're trying to weaken. They keep your mind occupied with sexual thoughts, tits, asses, f--king, getting off, hot chicks, etc. They make rebooting much harder and more painful.*
>
> *Either try to get laid (approach potential partners, set up dates, flirt, contact friends, go out) or do something completely unrelated to sex (work, study, exercise, hang out). The whole idea is to move away from that artificial/fantasy world and into the real world.*

Forcing sexual performance prematurely (ED)

Traditionally, both men and women assume that turning up the sexual heat is the solution to sexual sluggishness in a partner. However, those with porn-related sexual dysfunction often find that they heal faster if they allow their libido to reawaken naturally. In short, they need to reboot, free of sexual performance demands. One man described his girlfriend's support:

She has been so amazing. I told her that I would occasionally use porn fantasy to stay hard, and she told me that she'd rather I went soft than use porn. Knowing that actually made it easier, and I haven't even thought of porn since we had that convo a few weeks ago. She also refused to let me take any sort of ED drug, as she wanted me to sort this out naturally. Here's my advice:

1. Talk to your partner. It is by far the biggest help.

2. Take your time and go at a pace you are comfortable with.

3. Supplements had no effect what-so-ever.

4. Don't fall into the trap of looking at porn even if you don't plan to binge.

Funnily enough, my girlfriend went through a similar phase a while back of viewing too much porn and ending up finding that only girl-on-girl action would get her wet even though she is not lesbian at all. So she also had to give up the porn. This was good because she fully understood what I was going through.

Sure, we've had some lows. She's had some insecure feelings. I've had some terrible evenings of feeling inadequate and useless, but in the end we talked things through and came out stronger. Then, last weekend I managed to actually get and stay hard enough for sex. This is a huge step forward for me, the start of a new sexual adventure, and it's fantastic.

If orgasm sets off noticeable neurochemical ripples (the chaser) or sends you into a binge, don't push yourself to finish in the future. Keep your sexual activity gentle and low-key, that is, free of all performance pressure, while your sensitivity to pleasure returns naturally. It is better to leave wanting more than to exhaust your sexual desire.

If necessary, ask your partner not to play porn star in an effort to heat you up prematurely. Although dazzling foreplay and fantasy skills may produce the desired fireworks in the short-term, they can ultimately hamper healing. You can make up for lost time once you return to your studly self. The wait will be worth it:

> *Only a matter of weeks ago I had almost resigned myself to never being able to achieve climax during penetrative sex. Last night I had sex with my partner twice and reached climax both times! Once we started kissing and touching each other, I couldn't hold back on my urge to penetrate her. It felt so natural. The sensitivity in my penis has definitely returned, plus I feel there's more to come.*

Assuming a fetish is permanent

The belief that 'I can't help my fetishes; that's just who I am' can become a serious stumbling block to quitting internet porn because it can feel like you're abandoning your only hope of sexual fulfilment. The fact is, only by process of elimination will you know whether you are dealing with a porn-induced superficial 'fetish' or a true fetish arising from the core of your sexual identity.

Obviously, if a fetish disappears during the months after you quit porn then it wasn't integral to your sexual identity. In the meantime, your cravings for past highs related to your tastes in porn can deceive you. Said one young guy:

> *In summer 2011 I developed a new fetish, and oh god I could feel the dopamine in my brain. I was so happy and*

excited when watching this new type of porn that my body
would shake. Since then I have been a lot less happy and
have never gone back to normal.

Confused by the combination of past thrills and present dissatisfaction, some porn users escalate through a series of increasingly extreme porn. Others wonder if their sexual orientation has changed as they find new things intensely arousing and earlier things less arousing. Some desperately seek certainty by furiously masturbating to different kinds of porn in an effort to figure things out. Compulsive checking can drive them deep into an addiction or OCD-like behaviour without clarifying anything. Still others try acting out their fetishes in search of satisfaction.

In all cases, it makes sense to rule out excessive porn use as a cause *first.* The brain needs to rest not test. This is accomplished by quitting porn and porn fantasy for a few months. Watch out, because withdrawal discomfort or flatlining may persuade you that you just need more extreme scenarios to find satisfaction, when satisfaction actually lies in a balanced brain (the opposite direction). Addictive activity tends to fuel further activity rather than satiating it.[197] This forum member shared his experience:

Pornography made me able to become aroused only when
I imagined extreme images in my head. I did a lot of
extreme things with female prostitutes, but was left wholly
dissatisfied. Even with the transsexuals, nothing they did
aroused me. I had to force myself to become aroused by
thinking of extreme porn. I noticed that I was switching
between different sexual activities every few minutes at a
rate equal to how quickly I switched between porn videos
at home. During my porn use, I was unable to be turned
on simply by being near a naked woman (something I used
to love more than anything, and now love again). Today,

*after quitting porn, when I am intimate with a woman it's
an actual connection, an exceptional, awesome feeling. No
forced fantasies.*

Today's internet porn users are demonstrating that human
sexuality is far more malleable than anyone realized. Viewers
can use today's hyper-stimulating content to produce
supernormal arousal states, which they can maintain for hours.
As overconsumption leads to desensitization, the brain seeks
more dopamine via novelty, shock, forbidden content, kink,
seeking, etc. That's when earlier porn tastes may no longer do
the job.

Clearly there are early windows of development, during
which deep associations can get wired in more or less
permanently.

And of course, during puberty, all erotic memories gain
power, and are reinforced with each instance of arousal. Avid
porn use in teens, whose brains are highly plastic, can cause
sexual tastes to morph with surprising swiftness. Research
shows that the younger the age people first start to use porn,
the more likely they are to view bestiality or child porn.[198] In
an informal 2012 poll of (mostly young) people on r/nofap,
63% agreed that, 'My tastes became increasingly "extreme" or
"deviant"'.[199] Half were concerned; half weren't.

Yet porn fetishes often turn out to be superficial. Again,
many who quit porn (and porn-inspired fantasy) for a few
months see their extreme tastes dissipate.

The bad urge

The ideal time to deal with a bad urge is before it shows up.
When you first quit, plan ahead:

*Try to be home as little as possible. If you can't think of
anything to schedule for the first few days go to a library,
a bookstore or park to read. Not being at home, or a place*

where you usually fap, will be incredibly helpful in getting
past the first few days of withdrawal throes.

Make a list (now) of reasons you are avoiding porn and consult
it when The Urge arises. Better yet, write a note to yourself that
you can read when needed about what it will be like if you yield
to The Urge, just as this guy did:

You start some edging. Now there is no looking back. A little
more ... then a little more ... aaaand you're done. Most likely
the orgasm won't be very intense. You will feel a sense of relief
more than anything else. 'Now I can go back to my work', you
will say. 'That wasn't so bad. I don't feel any shame. There's
really no point denying yourself to such an extreme'.

When you sit down to work, it will be almost as if
nothing happened. In about an hour, you will start feeling
the energy drop, the onset of a mental fog. This will develop
into anxiety. The anxiety is not because of the fapping. It's
your natural response to the energy drop. Nothing bad
happened to you. No one told you off. You didn't have any
bad thoughts. Everything was ok until an hour ago. Now,
you're feeling slightly unwell. You can't concentrate so well.
You wish you didn't have to get any work done. You just feel
like sitting back and watching TV.

By the end of the day you will have not completed
your tasks for the day. Your defence mechanisms for
procrastination will kick in. Your mental state is now
completely at the mercy of external factors. How much
work can you accomplish the next day? Will you run into
any roadblocks? Depression kicks in. Your mind does not
want to engage with anything in case it makes things worse.
You don't want to meet people. Your brain is in shutdown
mode. You decide not to give in again.

Next, make a list of what you will do instead of use porn when

The Urge arises. Some people prepare by learning the 'Red X' technique:

> *I totally stopped fantasizing about porn about four weeks ago. Whenever a porn flashback enters my mind I visualise a big red X over it and imagine a loud ambulance siren. If the porn image is insistent, I visualise exploding it in my head. The key is to do it immediately. The technique becomes more automatic with time.*

If you don't know what else to do you can always wait and do nothing. Think to yourself, 'Here are cravings. They came out of nowhere and they have no real power over me. I am not my thoughts; I did not summon them; I do not want them; and I do not have to act on them.' Typically, the thought will vanish without a trace (for a time).

The fact is that all urges die down eventually, usually within quarter of an hour. And if you can get through The Bad Urge you can do anything, as this guy points out:

> *Once you learn that you are bigger than your urge and it always passes by, you'll be well on your way to ridding yourself of porn use. In my previous attempts, I would always give in to the one bad urge. Once I finally fought it I realized that I could fight any bad urge that comes. In that very moment when you feel you're weakest, when you feel like the urge is gonna defeat you, that's the moment in which you need to stay strong. On the other side of that urge is your breakthrough. When you beat that one bad urge, you realize you can beat them all. The key is to live one day at a time and stay diligent.*

Here are other tips that work for some people:

> *Don't discuss the situation with your brain. Your brain will*

try to rationalize porn use because it desperately wants it. The key here is not to argue with your own brain, but instead to simply acknowledge that you're having the thought, or to answer with one word: 'No'.

*

I just kinda hung my junk over in the sink and ladled cold water over it with my hands. It definitely kills the cravings. Also helps with blue balls.

*

I try to focus on drawing the sexual energy upward, into my chest and upper body to ease the pressure in my pants. It makes me feel really powerful. It relieves the need to masturbate, and kind of gives me this super 'ready for action' feeling. Like I could tear down a house if I needed to, or throw a girl around and have my way with her, in a consensual, playful way of course. I like it.

*

Do you keep giving yourself an excuse like 'I will do it one last time' or 'Today is the last time'? Change it to 'Just today I am not doing it'.

*

You will be able to go long periods of time without porn when watching porn is no longer an option in your life. Live as if porn didn't exist. Completely forget about it. Don't spend your day fighting urges. Don't 'try hard'. Be OK with the idea that you will never watch porn ever again in your life.

When The Urge shows up, and you feel like you have no control, turn off your device and think things through before acting on it. Even if you act on it afterward, you will do so consciously and that is the first step to changing behaviour.

Ultimately, the most important thing you can ever do is to never quit. I don't care if you reset every other day for a whole month or two. Even if that's the best you can do, you're now using porn half as often as you did. The most inspiring story I ever saw was of a guy who had a 15-day streak...after 3 whole years of trying. As long as you keep coming back, because you know how important it is for your own good, you cannot fail. It is only a matter of time until you reset your neural pathways and break free.

Common Questions

How long should I reboot?
Many websites that link to www.yourbrainonporn.com say it prescribes 60 or 90 days, or 8 weeks, etc. In fact, YBOP doesn't suggest any set amount of days, as the time is completely dependent on the severity of your porn-related problems, how your brain responds, and ***your goals.*** Time frames found in rebooting accounts on YBOP are all over the place because brains are different, and some men have stubborn porn-induced ED or DE.

Think of a reboot as discovering what is really you and what was porn-related, whether it be sexual dysfunctions, social anxiety, raging sex drive, ADD, depression, or whatever. Once you have a clear understanding of how you were affected by porn, you can steer your own ship.

Can I have sex during my reboot?
It's up to you. Some people find a temporary time-out from all sexual stimulation gives the brain a much needed rest and speeds recovery. On the other hand, daily affectionate touch is always beneficial, with or without sex. If you feel like the chaser effect is knocking you off balance after sex, you might try gentle lovemaking without the goal of orgasm for a while. It gives you the benefits of intimacy while still

allowing your brain to rest from intense sexual stimulation. However, if a reboot is taking a long time, some rebooters report that sex with a partner helps return their libido to normal.

If you think you are experiencing porn-induced ED, you may see better results if you don't force any sexual performance until you feel like your erections are arising spontaneously in the presence of your partner.

Should I reduce masturbation?
Not necessarily. You can try cutting out porn, porn fantasy and porn substitutes first. For some people that is enough to allow a return to balance. Others find that masturbation is a powerful trigger for activating porn pathways, so they do better if they give it a rest for a while.

> *Whenever I told myself I would only masturbate and never go back to porn, it wasn't long before masturbation became kind of boring to me. I would fantasize about real-life memories in the beginning, but my brain would quickly jump to memories from porn scenes and unrealistic fantasies. From there it would lead to erotic fiction, to amateur images, and then straight back to the hardcore porn videos.*

On the other hand, when porn-induced ED is present, the *majority* of men find that they need to drastically reduce masturbation and orgasm (temporarily). When you have a pathology, you usually need to do more than just eliminate the cause – in this case porn use. For example, you don't generally break a leg by putting weight on it. However, once it's broken you have to cast it, use crutches and eliminate walking while you heal. Same goes for porn-induced ED. You don't have to wear a cast, but you need to give your brain time to heal, free of intense sexual stimulation.

Note: You don't want to force yourself to masturbate using fantasy or other aids if it isn't yet happening spontaneously.

How do I know when I'm back to normal?
Obviously, there's no simple answer to this question as goals differ for each person. Common goals include: return of healthy erections, normalizing libido, diminishing of porn-induced fetishes, reversal of porn-induced sexual tastes, ease in managing cravings, and so forth. It's not uncommon for younger men to experience continued improvements long after the end of their rebooting phase.

These are some encouraging signs:

– You feel like flirting with potential mates, who look a lot more attractive.

– You are getting morning wood (or 'semis') frequently.

– You can orgasm without an intense chaser effect.

– Intercourse with a partner feels fantastic (Note: You may have a bit of premature ejaculation or delayed ejaculation early on. Practice makes perfect.)

– Your libido changes:

My libido went missing on and off for 6 months. Yet when it returned, it was a more wholesome libido. The desire for porn perving and sexually staring at woman disappeared completely.

Understandably, the men who reboot to reverse porn-induced ED tend to use their erectile health as a barometer.

How do I know that I don't just have a high libido?
Give up porn and porn fantasy and see what your libido is like some weeks later. It has been surprising to witness that most rebooters have an easier time eliminating masturbation *than*

they do porn. For many guys, masturbation is simply not that interesting without porn, and they are amazed to discover that porn, not high libido, was driving their constant search for relief.

Certainly, if you cannot masturbate without internet porn, or have a partially erect penis when you do, you are not horny or in need of 'release'. You are being driven by cravings. Your brain is seeking a fix: the relief of a temporary dopamine high.

How can I get excited by real partners? (ED)
Some young people started on internet porn early and wired themselves to screens and kink so thoroughly during adolescence that when they finally connect with a real partner they don't respond sexually. It can take months of no porn, porn fantasy or porn substitutes before their brains begin 'looking around' for other sexual stimuli and 'rewiring' to real people.

Obviously, it helps to spend time around real potential partners and limit all sexual fantasy to real people and realistic sexual scenarios. This young guy shared his strategy for 'rewiring':

> *I'm trying to put down a new pathway. I really want my brain to realize that the only way I get any sexual pleasure is through real women. If I don't actually have a sexual encounter with a real woman, I have to go to bed frustrated, and that's all there is to it. I don't allow myself to make up scenarios about women, but I do allow myself to reflect visually on women I have seen. Now, if I remember a woman's smile, I know that it's someone I met in real life. I have been going to bars and checking out/talking to women. Hopefully not in a creepy way. I get a good memory full of plenty of nice girls. Then I come home and just go to bed and try to sleep.*

Concluding Reflections

Nothing ever becomes real 'til it is experienced.

John Keats

If you suspect your porn use might be adversely affecting you, by all means make a simple experiment: Give it up for a time and see what you notice for yourself. There's no need to wait until experts reach a consensus. Quitting porn is not like engaging in an untested medical procedure or ingesting a risky pharmaceutical – situations where definitive research is not only possible but necessary.

Quitting internet porn is the equivalent of removing refined sugar or trans-fats from your diet. It is simply the elimination of a form of entertainment that no one had until recently, and everyone got along without. As one porn user said,

Here is the schema:
1. Exciting, but bad-in-long-term behaviour is introduced for money.
2. People get hooked.
3. Precise, scientifically backed-up research takes decades to kick-in.
4. Hooked people start to get educated.
5. They start behaviour-elimination.

Problem is that this whole cycle is so damaging. Cigarettes were (widely) introduced in the early 20th century and took decades to regulate. We now know that certain types of foods are harmful. Yet, with food we are still in phase 2-3. Guess where we are with pornography? The useful scientific research is not even a few years old.

151

A consensus about the risks of high-speed internet porn could be decades off despite the efforts of urologists such as Cornell Medical School professor and author Harry Fisch, MD, who warns that too much porn use can make it 'significantly more difficult' to get aroused and stay aroused during real sex.[200] Most of society will need a lot longer to get up to speed.

A young psychiatrist, himself newly recovered from porn-induced sexual dysfunction,[201] pointed out that the internet porn phenomenon is only 10 or 15 years old, and way ahead of the research. He notes:

Medical research works at a snail's pace. With luck we'll be addressing this in 20 or 30 years ... when half the male population is incapacitated. Drug companies can't sell any medications by someone quitting porn.

We don't have to be quite that pessimistic. Even as I was writing this book, the first three brain studies on porn users appeared. All were excellent and published by highly respected journals. They aligned neatly with the self-reports I've been tracking for years. Yet, the massive informal experiment now going on in online forums (and summarized in this book) is some of the best evidence currently available on the effects of porn – and quitting porn.

There's much more to learn. But meanwhile, make your own experiment free of everyone else's agendas. As one ex-user wrote:

Once you've experienced the truth about porn for yourself you can no longer be deceived by propaganda about porn, whether it comes from the religious, the liberals or the porn producers. They all have their agendas, but you have knowledge and can create your own opinion based on what is best for you.

Understand the Science of Misinformation

If you're wondering why there's not yet a consensus on the effects of internet porn despite the swell of warnings, you may find the history of the Tobacco Wars instructive. Years ago, most everyone smoked including movie stars on screen. People loved puffing. It calmed the nerves, offered a predictable buzz and looked sophisticated. How could such a wonderful activity *really* be detrimental? Was nicotine *truly* addictive? When tar showed up in cadaver lungs incredulous smokers preferred to blame asphalt.

Causation studies could not be done because they would have entailed creating two random groups of people and asking one to smoke for years while the other refrained. Definitely unethical. Meanwhile, other kinds of evidence mounted that smoking was causing health problems and that people had great difficulty quitting: correlation studies, anecdotal reports from physicians and patients, etc. Prospective studies, which compare a group of similar subjects whose smoking habits differ, took decades.

During this time, studies fostered by the tobacco industry found no evidence of harm or addiction. Predictably, every time new evidence of harm appeared, the industry trotted out its 'studies' to create the impression that the authorities were in conflict – and that it was far too soon to quit smoking. For example, the head of the Tobacco Industry Research Committee said, 'If smoke in the lungs was a sure-fire cause of cancer we'd all have it. We'd all have had it long ago. The cause is much more complicated than that'. He also dismissed statistical connections as not proving 'causation'.

Ultimately, however, reality could not be denied. Smoking claimed more and more victims. At the same time, addiction research became more sophisticated and revealed the physiology of *how* nicotine produces addiction. In the end, the tobacco industry's spell was broken. These days, people still smoke but they do so knowing the risks. Efforts to paint a false picture about the harmlessness of smoking have ceased.

Meanwhile, much unnecessary damage had been done. Critically important health information, which should have taken a few years to become common knowledge, instead took decades – while fabricated uncertainty protected tobacco profits.

Big Tobacco's campaign to cast doubt on the link between smoking and disease is now a classic case study in a science called agnotology: *the study of the cultural production of ignorance.* Agnotology investigates the deliberate sowing of public misinformation and doubt in a scientific area. As Brian McDougal, the author of *Porned Out,* put it,

> *It's hard to imagine that a whole generation chain-smoked cigarettes without having any idea how harmful they are, but the same thing is happening today with online pornography.*

Is internet porn the new smoking? Almost all young men with internet access view porn and the percentages of women viewers are growing. Whenever something becomes the norm, there's an unexamined assumption that it must be harmless or 'normal', that is, that it cannot produce *abnormal* physiological results. However, that proved not to be the case with smoking.

And, just as with smoking, causality studies cannot be done. It would be unethical to create two groups of kids and keep one group as 'porn virgins' while setting the other group free on today's internet porn for years to see what percentage lose attraction to real partners, can't quit, or develop porn-induced sexual dysfunctions and extreme fetish tastes.

Studies that follow porn users and non-users over years may never be done, especially in those under 18. Even finding a group that doesn't use porn and another group who accurately report their porn usage would be quite challenging. In contrast, studying smoking was easy. You either smoked or you didn't, and you were perfectly happy to say what brand of cigarette, how many per day, and when you started.

Meanwhile, other kinds of evidence are mounting that some internet porn users experience severe problems. Researchers are reporting unprecedented ED in young men,[202][203][204] physicians are reporting that their patients recover after they give up internet porn,[205] and brain scientists are seeing worrisome brain changes even in moderate internet porn users[206] as well as porn addicts.[207] Addiction treatment facilities are seeing increases in internet porn-facilitated addiction. Lawyers are noting a rise of divorces in which internet porn use is a factor. Young people are reporting surprising changes in fetish-porn tastes, which often fade if they quit using.

In academia, dozens of correlation studies have been done on pornography's effects. Many reveal associations between internet porn use and depression, anxiety, social discomfort, relationship dissatisfaction, fetish tastes, etc. (Researchers have also correlated porn use in adolescents with negative health effects[208] and social isolation, conduct problems, delinquent behaviour, depression, and decreased emotional bonding with caregivers.[209]) In some men, porn use also correlates with abusive behaviour towards women.[210] Correlation does not amount to causation. But do we want to disregard possible side effects in pursuit of a nonessential activity like screen-induced climax?

At the same time, a small, vocal group of sexologists continues to insist that internet porn is harmless, or even beneficial, citing their own work. They dismiss correlation studies that contradict their views and call for 'double-blind studies' before they will take the alleged harms seriously.

While that sounds rigorously scientific – who, after all, could be against something as scientifically respectable as the 'double-blind'? – it is in fact profoundly silly. 'Double-blind' means that neither the investigator nor the subject knows that a variable has been altered. For example, neither knows who is receiving drug or placebo. 'Single-blind' means the investigator knows but the subject doesn't. It should be evident that neither type of study is possible in the case of porn use. The subject will always know that he or she has stopped using porn. If you hear anyone calling for 'double-blind studies' in this context you can be sure of one thing: they don't know what they're talking about.

As I say, the best causation experiment currently possible is being done right now by thousands of people in various online forums. Porn users are removing a single variable that they all have in common: porn use. This 'study' is not perfect. Other variables are also at work in their lives. But that would be equally true in a formal study testing the effects of, say, anti-depressants. Subjects will always have different diets, relationship situations, childhoods and so forth.

Some experts believe that porn-addiction deniers are not unlike the shills of the tobacco industry.[211] The difference is that their motives often appear to stem from uncritical 'sex positivity'. The deniers also deny the complaints of internet porn users experiencing unprecedented 'sex-negative' dysfunctions, such as delayed ejaculation or inability to orgasm during sex, erectile dysfunction and loss of attraction to real partners.

I am sceptical about the limited existing research that finds no evidence of harm from internet porn use for several reasons:

1. There is mounting hard science, that is, research by neuroscientists about internet addiction, porn use, and sex itself, which unravels the mystery of how chronic overconsumption causes predictable brain changes.

2. When internet addiction researchers investigated cause,[212] they found a *reversal* of addiction-related brain changes and symptoms after internet addicts stopped using. This is consistent with thousands of self-reports in online internet porn recovery forums.

3. Solid new research isolating the brains of internet porn users is now published,[213] [214] with more on the way. All of

the brain research on internet addictions (videogaming, gambling, social media, pornography) is lining up neatly with decades of substance addiction research. Addiction is addiction and neuroplasticity a fact of life.

4. In contrast, much sexology research that finds porn harmless is, on close inspection, flawed. The limited questions asked, the weight assigned to them, and how results are reported produce the illusion that more porn use equals greater benefits.[215]

Education – But What Kind?
What happened when researchers recently asked questions based on teens' reality instead of researchers' theories? The data promptly line up with the anecdotes in this book.

A new study on anal sex among men and women ages 16 to 18,[216] analysed a large qualitative sample from three diverse sites in England. Said the researchers: 'Few young men or women reported finding anal sex pleasurable and both expected anal sex to be painful for women.'

Why were couples engaging in anal sex if neither party found it pleasurable? 'The main reasons given for young people having anal sex were that men wanted to copy what they saw in pornography, and that "it's tighter". And "People must like it if they do it" (made alongside the seemingly contradictory expectation that it will be painful for women).'

This looks like a perfect example of adolescent brain training; 'This is how it's done; this is what I should do.' Also at work is a desire to boast to one's peers about being able to duplicate the acts seen in porn.

However, as hypothesized in the Max Planck study,[217] today's porn users may also be seeking more 'edgy' sexual practices and more intense stimulation ('tighter') due to reduced sensitivity to pleasure. In the latter event, teens need more than 'discussions of pleasure, pain, consent and coercion' (recommended by the anal-sex researchers). They need to learn how chronic overstimulation can alter their brains and tastes.

Already, teens are figuring out that porn is having unwanted effects on their lives. A June, 2014 poll of 18-year olds from across the UK[218] found the following:

– Pornography can be addictive: Agree: 67% Disagree: 8%

– Pornography can have a damaging impact on young people's views of sex or relationships: Agree: 70% Disagree: 9%

– Pornography has led to pressure on girls or young women to act a certain way: Agree: 66% Disagree: 10%

– Pornography leads to unrealistic attitudes toward sex: Agree: 72% Disagree: 7%

– There's nothing wrong with watching pornography: Agree: 47% Disagree: 19%

Is it possible that the teens who grew up with streaming porn and then watched the effects of smartphones on themselves and their peers know more about the impact of internet porn than those who are endeavouring to educate them? Only 19% of teens saw something wrong with watching pornography, but more than two thirds perceived porn's harmful effects. These results suggest that many young people don't fit into the accepted frame for debates about porn. They don't think it's wrong to watch pornography. That is, they (presumably) don't reject it on puritanical grounds or out of 'sex negative' shame. Yet many of those who have no objection to porn as such can see that it causes serious problems. We need to listen to today's users and their peers because the phenomenon is moving so fast.

It seems futile to try to keep adolescents away from explicit material altogether and recklessly irresponsible not to inform them properly about its potential for harm.

So what do we do to prepare (potential) porn users so, like smokers, they can make informed choices? Perhaps you've heard that education is the solution. I agree, but such education needs to inform all ages of the symptoms that today's internet porn users are reporting, as well as teach people how the brain learns, how chronic overconsumption can alter it for the worse, and what is entailed in reversing unwanted brain changes (sexual conditioning, addiction).

Furthermore, everyone can benefit from knowledge of how the primitive appetite mechanism of the brain, the reward circuitry, has priorities set by evolution: furthering survival and genetic success. It votes 'Yes!' for more calories or more 'fertilization' opportunities regardless of the potential consequences.

People also need to know that reward-circuitry balance is indispensable for lifelong emotional, physical and mental wellbeing because of its power to shape our perceptions and choices without our conscious awareness. And to be informed of methods that help humans steer for balance in the reward circuitry: exercise and other beneficial stressors, time in nature, companionship, healthy relationships, meditation and so on.

Once we begin to think clearly about neuroplasticity we are inevitably drawn to the question of what we want from life – what we consider to be a good life. Each of us must answer that for ourselves. But we are best able to do so when we understand the threats that some substances and behaviours pose to our capacity to live the lives we want. Self-determination requires that we understand ourselves as best we can.

When we are dealing with young people we have an even greater responsibility to understand the risks that explicit sexual material can pose. Adolescents cannot decide for themselves what constitutes the good life and there are grounds for thinking that disruption of their reward-circuits can take more of a toll than in adults. So I would also like to see widespread education about the unique vulnerabilities of the adolescent brain with respect to sexual conditioning and addiction.

Instead, you sometimes hear that schools only need to teach kids how to distinguish 'good porn' from 'bad porn'. For example, in 2013 the *Daily Mail* proclaimed, 'teachers should give lessons in pornography and tell pupils "it's not all bad", experts say'. The claim is that all one needs to know to enjoy both is the difference between fantasy and reality.

Sadly, there is not one shred of scientific evidence to support the idea that pointing kids to 'good porn' will prevent problems or prepare them for today's hyperstimulating environment. Such thinking actually runs counter to dozens of internet-addiction brain science studies, which suggest that the internet itself – that is, the delivery on demand of endless enticing stimulation – is the chief peril. Porn users can keep their dopamine at artificially high levels for hours simply by clicking. Even if they confine their excursions to 'good porn', they still risk conditioning their sexual response to screens, voyeurism, isolation and the ability to click to more stimulation at will. Two porn users comment:

> *Videos and pornography don't do it for me. The fake look of porn and porn actresses turns me off. I just use stills of athletic women. But I'm looking for that right girl or image that gets me off, so I view hundreds per session. My current girlfriend actually fits what I would masturbate to. While I'm very attracted to her I'm noticing weak erections. I believe my brain rewired to the 'searching' aspect as well as the variety and the comfort of not having to please anyone but myself.*

*

> *I tried to heal my porn problems by changing what types of porn I watched. I avoided all professional porn, sticking*

*to homemade stuff, which at least has 'real girls'. Of course
half that stuff is fake and involves porn stars anyway. And,
I still spent hours finding the 'perfect' clip to finish with,
meanwhile giving my brain endless hits.*

Watching 'good porn' won't eradicate these risks. For users whose
brains easily go out of balance in response to overstimulation,
there is no 'good' porn, with the possible exception of an old-
fashioned magazine. For them, the unending erotic novelty of
the internet comprises a supernormal stimulus.

As a matter of science, an attempt to sort good porn from
bad is futile. The brain's reward circuitry, which drives sexual
arousal, has no definition of 'porn'. It just sends a 'go get it!'
signal in response to whatever releases sufficient dopamine.

It should also be evident that teaching 'realistic sex' doesn't
stop teens from accessing extreme content when left (literally)
to their own devices. Teen brains evolved with a penchant for
the weird and wonderful; they are powerfully drawn to novelty
and surprise. Such a naive policy would be like handing a teen
an old issue of *Playboy* and telling him that the only suitable
content is on pages 5 through 18. As a teen, which pages would
you have turned to first?

Incidentally, the good-porn-bad-porn proposal may arise
from less than noble intent. It lays the groundwork for endless
debate about *values*. It is an invitation for the most vocal to
lobby for the suitability of their preferred types of porn while
maintaining that critics are trying to impose their arbitrary
moral standards. What any group thinks is bad another will
argue is vital.

Yet frankly, type of content and orientation of the viewer
may be of little import compared with today's delivery. Since
the advent of streaming clips of porn videos, escalating,
morphing sexual tastes, a range of sexual dysfunctions and loss
of attraction to real partners appear to be affecting a percentage
of all groups: gay, straight and in between. It is the way that

users can maintain a prolonged dopamine high from endless novel content that seems to create the problem.

Debates about good and bad porn are beyond the realm of science and can never be resolved. Meanwhile, they distract everyone from the mounting scientific evidence, and still needed research, on internet porn's actual effects on users. Let's steer the debate away from unscientific distractions and back to the effects on porn users and the hard science that helps explain what they're experiencing. In the process, we can all learn a lot about human sexuality.

In the end, such a focus will also serve porn users. Like smokers, they will be able to make informed choices about pornography use with full knowledge of its risks for plastic brains like ours.

We are what we repeatedly do. Aristotle

Further Reading

Burnham, Terry and Phelan, Jay, *Mean Genes: From Sex to Money to Food Taming Our Primal Instincts,* New York: Basic Books, 2000. Funny, informative book about how the reward circuitry of the brain drives us to do things that are not always in our best interests.

Chamberlain, Mark, PhD and Geoff Steurer MS, LMFT, *Love You, Hate the Porn: Healing a Relationship Damaged by Virtual Infidelity,* Salt Lake City: Shadow Mountain, 2011. Practical guide for married couples where one partner was deeply upset by the other partner's porn use.

Church, Noah B.E., *Wack: Addicted to Internet Porn,* Portland: Bvrning Qvestions, LLC, 2014. Brilliant, readable, personal account of a 24-year old who recovered from porn-related sexual dysfunction.

Doidge, Norman, MD, *The Brain That Changes Itself,* New York: Viking, 2007. Fascinating book about brain plasticity, with a chapter on sex and porn.

Fisch, Harry, MD, *The New Naked: The Ultimate Sex Education for Grown-Ups,* Naperville: Sourcebooks, Inc. 2014. Standard-issue self-help book for couples with porn-related problems.

Hall, Paula, *Understanding and Treating Sex Addiction: A Comprehensive Guide For People Who Struggle With Sex Addiction And Those Who Want To Help Them,* East Sussex: Routledge, 2013. Practical guide for therapists and porn-afflicted alike by UK therapist.

McDougal, Brian, *Porned Out: Erectile Dysfunction, Depression, And 7 More (Selfish) Reasons To Quit Porn,* Kindle ebook, 2012. Brief, useful book by recovered porn user.

Maltz, Wendy, LCSW, DST and Larry Maltz, *The Porn Trap: The Essential Guide to Overcoming Problems Caused by Pornography,* New York: Harper, 2010. Practical guide for therapists and porn-afflicted alike by US therapists.

Robinson, Marnia, *Cupid's Poisoned Arrow: From Habit to Harmony in Sexual Relationships,* Berkeley: North Atlantic Books, 2011. Discusses the effects of sex on the brain and relationships, with a chapter on porn.

Toates, Frederick, *How Sexual Desire Works: The Enigmatic Urge*, Cambridge: Cambridge University Press, 2014. Toates, Emeritus Professor of Biological Psychology at The Open University, outlines the relevance of neuroplasticity for nearly every aspect of human sexuality, addiction included.

Notes

[1] Note number of "Fapstronauts" on Reddit and post by Chinese visitor about similar site, "Chinese way of nofap," http://www.reddit.com/r/NoFap/comments/28smcs/chinese_way_of_nofap.

[2] Jason S. Carroll, et al., "Generation XXX: Pornography Acceptance and Use Among Emerging Adults," *Journal of Adolescent Research,* 23/1 (2008), doi: 10.1177/0743558407306348.

[3] Chyng Sun, Ana Bridges, Jennifer Johnason and Matt Ezzell, "Pornography and the Male Sexual Script An Analysis of Consumption and Sexual Relations," *Archives of Sexual Behavior,* (December, 2014), http://link.springer.com/article/10.1007%2Fs10508-014-0391-2.

[4] "LIVE BLOG. Porn-Induced erectile dysfunction and young men," *16x9* (TV), March 31, 2014, http://globalnews.ca/news/1232800/live-blog-porn-induced-erectile-dysfunction-and-young-men.

[5] Harry Fisch, MD, *The New Naked: The Ultimate Sex Education for Grown-Ups* Fisch, Naperville: Sourcebooks, Inc. 2014.

[6] Simone Kühn and Jürgen Gallinat, "Brain Structure and Functional Connectivity Associated With Pornography Consumption: The Brain on Porn," *JAMA Psychiatry* (2014), doi:10.1001/jamapsychiatry.2014.93.

[7] Valerie Voon, et al., "Neural Correlates of Sexual Cue Reactivity in Individuals with and without Compulsive Sexual Behaviours", *PLOS One* (2014): DOI: 10.1371/journal.pone.0102419.

[8] H. Mouras, et al., " Activation of mirror-neuron system by erotic video clips predicts degree of induced erection: an fMRI study," *Neuroimage.* 42(3) (2008): 1142-50, doi: 10.1016/j.neuroimage.2008.05.051.

[9] M. Brand, et al. "Watching pornographic pictures on the Internet: role of sexual arousal ratings and psychological-psychiatric symptoms for using Internet sex sites excessively," *Cyberpsychol Behav Soc Netw* 14/6 (2011): 371-377, doi: 10.1089/cyber.2010.0222.

[10] Sherry Pagoto, PhD, "What Do Porn and Snickers Have in Common?" *Psychology Today* blogs, August 7, 2012, http://www.psychologytoday.com/blog/shrink/201208/what-do-porn-and-snickers-have-in-common.

[11] Links to Chinese forums: http://www.jiese.org/bbs/index.php and

http://tieba.baidu.com. Also see this forum post, "Chinese way of nofap" June 22, 2014, http://www.reddit.com/r/NoFap/comments/28smcs/chinese_way_of_nofap.

[12] G. Rodríguez-Manzo, I.L. Guadarrama-Bazante, A. Morales-Calderón, "Recovery from sexual exhaustion-induced copulatory inhibition and drug hypersensitivity follow a same time course: two expressions of a same process?" *Behav Brain Res* 217/2 (2011): 253-260, doi: 10.1016/j.bbr.2010.09.014.

[13] John J. Medina, PhD, "Of Stress and Alcoholism, Of Mice and Men," *Psychiatric Times*, July, 2008, 18-19.

[14] http://www.reddit.com/r/NoFap; http://www.rebootnation.org; http://www.reddit.com/r/pornfree; http://www.yourbrainrebalanced.com; http://www.nofap.org.

[15] NoFap Survey, *www.reddit.com/r/NoFap*, March, 2014, https://docs.google.com/file/d/0B7q3tr4EV02wbkpTTVk4R2VGbm8/edit?pli=1.

[16] Nathaniel M. Lambert, *et al.*, "A Love That Doesn't Last: Pornography Consumption and Weakened Commitment to One's Romantic Partner," *Journal of Social and Clinical Psychology* 31/4 (2012): 410-438.

[17] Michael E. Levin, Jason Lillis, Steven C. Hayes, "When is Online Pornography Viewing Problematic Among College Males? Examining the Moderating Role of Experiential Avoidance," *Sexual Addiction & Compulsivity* 19/3 (2012): 168-180, doi: 10.1080/10720162.2012.657150.

[18] E.M. Morgan, "Associations between young adults' use of sexually explicit materials and their sexual preferences, behaviors, and satisfaction," *J Sex Res* 48/6 (2011): 520-530, doi: 10.1080/00224499.2010.543960.

[19] J.B. Weaver 3rd, *et. al.,* " Mental- and physical-health indicators and sexually explicit media use behavior by adults," *J Sex Med.* 8/3 (2011): 764-72, doi: 10.1111/j.1743-6109.2010.02030.x.

[20] Andreas G. Philaretou, Ahmed Y. Mahfouz, Katherine R. Allen, "Use of internet pornography and men's well-being," *Men's Studies Press* 4/2 (2005): 149-169, doi 10.3149/jmh.0402.149.

[21] Kat Daine, *et al.*, "The Power of the Web: A Systematic Review of Studies of the Influence of the Internet on Self-Harm and Suicide in Young People," *PLoS One,* October 30, 2013, doi: 10.1371/journal.pone.0077555.

[22] Carlo Foresta, "Progetto ANDROLIFE: Salute e Sesso," February 21, 2014, http://www.associazionevenetoesalute.it/www.associazionevenetoesalute.it/uploads/foresta.pdf.

[23] Elisa Fais, "Diciottenni consumatori abituali di spinelli e cyber sex,"

Il Mattino di Padova, December 1, 2014, http://mattinopadova.gelocal.it/padova/cronaca/2014/12/01/news/diociottenni-consumatori-abituali-di-spinelli-e-cyber-sex-1.10414447

[24] Carlo Foresta, "Progetto ANDROLIFE: Salute e Sesso," February 21, 2014, http://www.associazionevenetoesalute.it/www.associazionevenetoesalute.it/uploads/foresta.pdf.

[25] Armed Forces Health Surveillance Center, "Erectile dysfunction among male active component service members, U.S. Armed Forces, 2004–2013," *MSMR,* 21.9 (2014): 13-6.

[26] Matt Purple, "Rare Under-40 Poll: Porn is ruining our sex lives?" *Rare,* September 18, 2014, http://rare.us/story/one-third-of-young-people-say-porn-is-ruining-their-sex-lives/

[27] Lucia F. O'Sullivan, *et al.,* "Prevalence and Characteristics of Sexual Functioning among Sexually Experienced Middle to Late Adolescents," *J Sex Med* 11/3 (2014): 630-641, doi: 10.1111/jsm.12419.

[28] Valerie Voon, *et al.,* "Neural Correlates of Sexual Cue Reactivity in Individuals with and without Compulsive Sexual Behaviours", *PLOS One* (2014): DOI: 10.1371/journal.pone.0102419.

[29] Gregory Z Tau and Bradley S Peterson, "Normal Development of Brain Circuits," *Neuropsychopharmacology* 35/1 (2010): 147–168, doi: 10.1038/npp.2009.115.

[30] Dolf Zillmann, "Shifting Preferences in Pornography Consumption," *Communication Research,* 13/4 (1986): 560-578, doi: 10.1177/009365086013004003.

[31] Dolf Zillmann, "Effects of Prolonged Consumption of Pornography," Paper Prepared for the Surgeon General's Workshop on Pornography and Public Health, (1986) http://130.14.81.99/ps/access/NNBCKV.pdf.

[32] Sharlene A. Wolchik *et al.,* "The effect of emotional arousal on subsequent sexual arousal in men," *Journal of Abnormal Psychology* 89/4 (1980): 595-598.

[33] "Why a hungry man loves a curvy woman," *IOL Lifestyle,* June 6, 2014, http://www.iol.co.za/lifestyle/style/beauty/why-a-hungry-man-loves-a-curvy-woman-1.1699654.

[34] Mirte Brom, Stephanie Both, Ellen Laan, Walter Everaerd and Philip Spinhoven, "The role of conditioning, learning and dopamine in sexual behavior: A narrative review of animal and human studies," *Neuroscience and Biobehavioral Reviews* 11 (2013), DOI: 10.1016/j.neubiorev.2013.10.014.

[35] Karolina Müller, *et al.,* "Changes in Sexual Arousal as Measured by

Penile Plethysmography in Men with Pedophilic Sexual Interest," *J Sex Med* 11 (2014): 1221-1229, doi: 10.1111/jsm.12488.

[36] Yuri Tomikawa, "No Sex, Please, We're Young Japanese Men," *The Wall Street Journal,* January 13, 2011.

[37] Henry Samuel, "French women 'are the sexual predators now'," *The Telegraph,* March 7, 2008.

[38] Chyng Sun, Ana Bridges, Jennifer Johnason and Matt Ezzell, "Pornography and the Male Sexual Script An Analysis of Consumption and Sexual Relations," *Archives of Sexual Behavior,* (December, 2014), http://link. springer.com/article/10.1007%2Fs10508-014-0391-2.

[39] Yan Liu *et al.,* "Nucleus accumbens dopamine mediates amphetamine-induced impairment of social bonding in a monogamous rodent species," *PNAS,* 107/3 (2009): 1217–1222, doi: 10.1073/pnas.0911998107.

[40] Jennifer Viegas, "Flirty strangers sway how men see partners," *Discovery News/ABC Science,* March 26, 2007, http://www.abc.net.au/science/articles/2007/03/26/1881621.htm.

[41] Dolf Zillmann and Jennings Bryant, "Pornography's Impact on Sexual Satisfaction," *Journal of Applied Social Psychology* 18/5 (1988): 438–453, doi: 10.1111/j.1559-1816.1988.tb00027.x.

[42] Stephanie S. Luster, " Emerging Adult Sexual Attitudes and Behaviors: Does Shyness Matter?" *Emerging Adulthood* 1/3 (2013): 185-195, doi: 10.1177/2167696813475611.

[43] Vincent Cyrus Yoder ; Thomas B. Virden III ; Kiran Amin, " Internet Pornography and Loneliness: An Association?" *Sexual Addiction & Compulsivity,* 12/1 (2005): 19-44.

[44] Matthias Brand, Kimberly S. Young and Christian Laier, " Prefrontal control and Internet addiction: a theoretical model and review of neuropsychological and neuroimaging findings," *Frontiers in Human Neuroscience* 8/375 (2014), doi: 10.3389/fnhum.2014.00375.

[45] E. Dalbudak and C. Evren, "The relationship of Internet addiction severity with Attention Deficit Hyperactivity Disorder symptoms in Turkish University students; impact of personality traits, depression and anxiety," *Compr Psychiatry,* 55/3 (2014): 497-503, doi: 10.1016/j.comppsych.2013.11.018.

[46] Simone Kühn and Jürgen Gallinat, "Brain Structure and Functional Connectivity Associated With Pornography Consumption: The Brain on Porn," *JAMA Psychiatry* (2014), doi:10.1001/jamapsychiatry.2014.93.

[47] Andrew Myers, "Researchers both induce, relieve depression symptoms

in mice by stimulating single brain region with light," *Stanford School of Medicine*, December 12, 2012, http://med.stanford.edu/ism/2012/december/deisseroth.html.

[48] M. Walter *et al.*, "Distinguishing specific sexual and general emotional effects in fMRI-subcortical and cortical arousal during erotic picture viewing," *Neuroimage* 40/4 (2008): 1482-1494. doi: 10.1016/j.neuroimage.2008.01.040.

[49] J.G. Pfaus, "Dopamine: helping males copulate for at least 200 million years: theoretical comment on Kleitz-Nelson et al," *Behav Neurosci* 124/6 (2010): 877-880; discussion 881-3, doi: 10.1037/a0021823.

[50] F. Giuliano, J. Allard, "Dopamine and male sexual function," *Eur Urol* 40/6 (2001): 601-608

[51] R.A. Wise, "Dual roles of dopamine in food and drug seeking: the drive-reward paradox," *Biol Psychiatry* 73/9 (2013): 819-826, doi: 10.1016/j.biopsych.2012.09.001.

[52] James G. Pfaus and Lisa A. Scepkowski, "The Biologic Basis for Libido," *Current Sexual Health Reports* 2/2 (2005): 95-100, 10.1007/s11930-005-0010-2.

[53] Kimberly A. Young, Kyle L. Gobrogge, Yan Liu, and Zuoxin Wang "The neurobiology of pair bonding: insights from a socially monogamous rodent," *Front Neuroendocrinol* 32/1 (2011): 53–69, doi: 10.1016/j.yfrne.2010.07.006.

[54] J.R. Parkitna, *et al.*, "Novelty-seeking behaviors and the escalation of alcohol drinking after abstinence in mice are controlled by metabotropic glutamate receptor 5 on neurons expressing dopamine d1 receptors," *Biol Psychiatry* 73/3 (2013): 263-270, doi: 10.1016/j.biopsych.2012.07.019.

[55] Natalie Angier, "A Molecule of Motivation, Dopamine Excels at Its Task," *The New York Times,* October 26, 2009, http://www.nytimes.com/2009/10/27/science/27angier.html.

[56] Cathleen Genova, "Learning addiction: Dopamine reinforces drug-associated memories," research press release, September 9, 2009, http://www.eurekalert.org/pub_releases/2009-09/cp-lad090309.php.

[57] John D. Salamone and Mercè Correa, "The Mysterious Motivational Functions of Mesolimbic Dopamine," *Neuron* 76/3 (2012): 470–485, http://dx.doi.org/10.1016/j.neuron.2012.10.021.

[58] Robert Sapolsky, "Dopamine Jackpot! Sapolsky on the Science of Pleasure," FORA TV, February 1, 2012, http://www.dailymotion.com/video/xh6ceu_dopamine-jackpot-sapolsky-on-the-science-of-pleasure_news.

[59] Bridget M. Kuehn, "Willingness to Work Hard Linked to Dopamine Response in Brain Regions," *News@JAMA,* May 2, 2012, http://newsatjama.

jama.com/2012/05/02/willingness-to-work-hard-linked-to-dopamine-response-in-brain-regions; and Lisa Franchi, "Dopamine Keeps the Brain Motivated to Pursue a Distant Goal," *NaturalTherapyForAll.com*, August 07, 2013, http://blog.naturaltherapyforall.com/2013/08/07/dopamine-keeps-the-brain-motivated-to-pursue-a-distant-goal.

⁶⁰ Kent C Berridge, Terry E. Robinson, J. Wayne Aldridge, "Dissecting components of reward: 'liking', 'wanting', and learning," *Curr Opin Pharmacol* 9/1 (2009): 65–73, doi: 10.1016/j.coph.2008.12.014.

⁶¹ Susan Weinschenk, "100 Things You Should Know About People: #8 — Dopamine Makes You Addicted To Seeking Information," *Brain Lady Blog*, November 7, 2009, http://www.blog.theteamw.com/2009/11/07/100-things-you-should-know-about-people-8-dopamine-makes-us-addicted-to-seeking-information.

⁶² Terry E Robinson and Kent C Berridge, "The incentive sensitization theory of addiction: some current issues," *Phil. Trans. R. Soc. B* 363 (2008): 3137–3146, doi:10.1098/rstb.2008.0093.

⁶³ Cell Press, "Pure Novelty Spurs The Brain." *ScienceDaily*, 27 August 2006, www.sciencedaily.com/releases/2006/08/060826180547.htm.

⁶⁴ E. Koukounas and B. Over, "Changes in the magnitude of the eyeblink startle response during habituation of sexual arousal," *Behav Res Ther*, 38/6 (2000): 573-584

⁶⁵ I. Meuwissen and R. Over, "Habituation and dishabituation of female sexual arousal," *Behaviour Research and Therapy* 28/3 (1990): 217-226, doi: 10.1016/0005-7967(90)90004-3.

⁶⁶ Max Miller, "Big Think Interview With Adam Kepecs," *BigThink.com*, August 20, 2010, http://bigthink.com/videos/big-think-interview-with-adam-kepecs.

⁶⁷ David H. Barlow, David K. Sakheim, J. Gayle Beck, "Anxiety increases sexual arousal," *Journal of Abnormal Psychology* 92/1 (1983): 49-54.

⁶⁸ Bianca C. Wittmann, Nico Bunzeck, Raymond J. Dolan, and Emrah Düzel, "Anticipation of novelty recruits reward system and hippocampus while promoting recollection," *Neuroimage* 38/1-9 (2007): 194–202, doi: 10.1016/j.neuroimage.2007.06.038.

⁶⁹ Stuart McMillen, "Supernormal Stimuli," *www.highexistence.com*, December, 2011, http://www.highexistence.com/supernatural-stimuli-comic.

⁷⁰ "How Technology is Like Bug Sex," *www.nirandfar.com*, http://www.nirandfar.com/2013/01/how-technology-is-like-bug-sex.html.

⁷¹ Robert O. Deaner, Amit V. Khera, and Michael L. Platt, "Monkeys Pay

Per View: Adaptive Valuation of Social Images by Rhesus Macaques," *Current Biology* 15 (2005): 543–548, doi 10.1016/j.cub.2005.01.044.

[72] R.M. Krebs, D. Heipertz, H. Schuetze, E. Duzel, "Novelty increases the mesolimbic functional connectivity of the substantia nigra/ventral tegmental area (SN/VTA) during reward anticipation: Evidence from high-resolution fMRI," *Neuroimage* 58/2 (2011): 647-55, doi: 10.1016/j.neuroimage.2011.06.038.

[73] J. Spicer, *et al.*, "Sensitivity of the nucleus accumbens to violations in expectation of reward," *Neuroimage* 34/1 (2007): 455-461.

[74] "Robot Handjobs Are The Future, And The Future Is Coming," *HuffPost Live*, November 13, 2013, http://live.huffingtonpost.com/r/archive/segment/robot-handjobs-are-the-future-and-the-future-is-coming/5283e961fe34444eb70002bd.

[75] Robert Weiss, "Techy-Sexy: Digital Exploration of the Erotic Frontier," *Psychology Today* blogs, November 18, 2013, http://www.psychologytoday.com/blog/love-and-sex-in-the-digital-age/201311/techy-sexy-digital-exploration-the-erotic-frontier.

[76] "The FriXion Revolution," *YouTube*, November 18, 2013, https://www.youtube.com/watch?v=haBM4GFu9Bs.

[77] P.J. Kenny, G. Voren and P.M. Johnson, " Dopamine D2 receptors and striatopallidal transmission in addiction and obesity," *Curr Opin Neurobiol*, 23/4 (2013): 535-538, doi: 10.1016/j.conb.2013.04.012. This has been confirmed by German researchers Simone Kühn and Jürgen Gallinat, "Brain Structure and Functional Connectivity Associated With Pornography Consumption: The Brain on Porn," *JAMA Psychiatry* (2014), doi:10.1001/jamapsychiatry.2014.93.

[78] "Porn vs Reality - TheSite.org," *YouTube*, May 28, 2012, https://www.youtube.com/watch?v=L9BPbe9_Jsw.

[79] James G. Pfaus, *et al.*, "Who, What, Where, When (and Maybe Even Why)? How the Experience of Sexual Reward Connects Sexual Desire, Preference, and Performance," *Arch Sex Behav* 41 (2012): 31–62, doi 10.1007/s10508-012-9935-5.

[80] T. Tydén and C. Rogala, "Sexual behaviour among young men in Sweden and the impact of pornography," *Int J STD AIDS* 15/9 (2004): 590-593.

[81] Paul R. A. Stokes, et al., "Nature or Nurture? Determining the Heritability of Human Striatal Dopamine Function: an [18F]-DOPA PET Study," *Neuropsychopharmacology*, 38 (2013): 485–491, doi:10.1038/npp.2012.207.

[82] Valerie Voon, *et al.*, "Neural Correlates of Sexual Cue Reactivity in

Individuals with and without Compulsive Sexual Behaviours", *PLOS One* (2014): doi: 10.1371/journal.pone.0102419.

[83] L.D. Selemon, "A role for synaptic plasticity in the adolescent development of executive function," *Transl Psychiatry*, 3/3 (2013): e238, doi: 10.1038/tp.2013.7.

[84] Daniel R. Weinberger, Brita Elvevåg and Jay N. Giedd, "The Adolescent Brain: A Work in Progress," *The National Campaign To Prevent Teen Pregnancy*, 2005, http://web.calstatela.edu/faculty/dherz/Teenagebrain.workinprogress.pdf.

[85] "Best memory? You're likely to decide as a teen," *Medical Xpress*, July 20, 2012, http://medicalxpress.com/news/2012-07-memory-youre-teen.html.

[86] Karla S. Frohmader *et al.*, "Methamphetamine acts on subpopulations of neurons regulating sexual behavior in male rats," *Neuroscience* 166/3 (2010): 771–784, doi: 10.1016/j.neuroscience.2009.12.070.

[87] K.K. Pitchers, *et al.*, "Endogenous opioid-induced neuroplasticity of dopaminergic neurons in the ventral tegmental area influences natural and opiate reward," *J Neurosci* 34/26 (2014): 8825-8836, doi: 10.1523/JNEUROSCI.0133-14.2014.

[88] Kyle K. Pitchers, *et al.*, "Natural and Drug Rewards Act on Common Neural Plasticity Mechanisms with DeltaFosB as a Key Mediator," *J Neurosci* 33/8 (2013): 3434–3442, doi: 10.1523/JNEUROSCI.4881-12.2013.

[89] Christopher M. Olsen, "Natural Rewards, Neuroplasticity, and Non-Drug Addictions," *Neuropharmacology* 61/7 (2011): 1109–1122, doi: 10.1016/j.neuropharm.2011.03.010.

[90] Bonnie K. Lee and Madison Moore, "Shame and Sex Addiction: Through A Cinematic Lens," *J Addict Behav Ther Rehabil* 3/1 (2014), http://dx.doi.org/10.4172/2324-9005.1000116.

[91] Paul M. Johnson and Paul J. Kenny, " Addiction-like reward dysfunction and compulsive eating in obese rats: Role for dopamine D2 receptors," *Nat Neurosci*, 13/5 (2010): 645-641, doi: 10.1038/nn.2519.

[92] Maia Szalavitz, "Can Food Really Be Addictive? Yes, Says National Drug Expert," *Time*, April 05, 2012, http://healthland.time.com/2012/04/05/yes-food-can-be-addictive-says-the-director-of-the-national-institute-on-drug-abuse.

[93] Mark Hyman, MD, "Food Addiction: Could It Explain Why 70 Percent of Americans Are Fat?," *HuffPost Healthy Living*, October 16, 2010, http://www.huffingtonpost.com/dr-mark-hyman/food-addiction-could-it-e_b_764863.html.

[94] K. Blum, Y. Liu, R. Shriner, M.S. Gold, "Reward circuitry dopaminergic

activation regulates food and drug craving behavior," *Curr Pharm Des*17/12 (2011): 1158-1167.

[95] Sarah Klein, "Fatty foods may cause cocaine-like addiction," *CNN Health*, March 30, 2010, http://www.cnn.com/2010/HEALTH/03/28/fatty.foods.brain.

[96] Magalie Lenoir, Fuschia Serre, Lauriane Cantin, Serge H. Ahmed, "Intense Sweetness Surpasses Cocaine Reward," *PLoS One*, August 01, 2007, doi: 10.1371/journal.pone.0000698.

[97] "Prevalence of Overweight and Obesity," *Centers for Disease Control and Prevention, National Health and Nutrition Examination Survey*, 2009-2010, http://win.niddk.nih.gov/statistics/#b.

[98] ProvenMen.org Pornography Addiction Survey (conducted by Barna Group), "Frequency of Pornography Viewing by Men," 2014, http://www.provenmen.org/2014pornsurvey/pornography-use-and-addiction/#addiction

[99] Deirdre Barrett, "Supernormal Stimuli," *HuffPost Books*, June 16, 2010, http://www.huffingtonpost.com/deirdre-barrett/supernormal-stimuli_b_613466.html.

[100] Eric J. Nestler, "DeltaFosB: a Molecular Switch for Reward," *Journal of Drug and Alcohol Research*, 2 (2013), doi:10.4303/jdar/235651.

[101] "Internet & Video Game Addiction Brain Studies," *www.yourbrainonporn.com*, http://yourbrainonporn.com/list-internet-video-game-brain-studies.

[102] G.J. Meerkerk, R.J. Van Den Eijnden, H. E. Garretsen, "Predicting compulsive Internet use: it's all about sex!" *Cyberpsychol Behav* 9/1 (2006): 95-103.

[103] Eric J. Nestler, "DeltaFosB: a Molecular Switch for Reward," *Journal of Drug and Alcohol Research* 2 (2013), doi:10.4303/jdar/235651.

[104] Michela Romano, Lisa A. Osborne, Roberto Truzoli, and Phil Reed, "Differential Psychological Impact of Internet Exposure on Internet Addicts," *PLoS One* 8/2 (2013) doi: 10.1371/journal.pone.0055162.

[105] Simone Kühn and Jürgen Gallinat, "Brain Structure and Functional Connectivity Associated With Pornography Consumption: The Brain on Porn," *JAMA Psychiatry* (2014), doi:10.1001/jamapsychiatry.2014.93.

[106] Brigitte Osterath, "Pea brain: watching porn online will wear out your brain and make it shrivel," *Deutsche Welle*, June 5, 2014, http://www.dw.de/pea-brain-watching-porn-online-will-wear-out-your-brain-and-make-it-shrivel/a-17681654.

[107] T.M. Zhu, *et al*, "Effects of electroacupuncture combined psycho-

intervention on cognitive function and event-related potentials P300 and mismatch negativity in patients with internet addiction," *Chin L Integr Med* 18/2 (2012), doi: 10.1007/s11655-012-0990-5.

[108] Valerie Voon, *et al.*, "Neural Correlates of Sexual Cue Reactivity in Individuals with and without Compulsive Sexual Behaviours", *PLOS One* (2014): doi: 10.1371/journal.pone.0102419.

[109] Daisy J. Mechelmans, et al., "Enhanced Attentional Bias towards Sexually Explicit Cues in Individuals with and without Compulsive Sexual Behaviours," *PLOS One*, (2014). DOI: 10.1371/journal.pone.0105476.

[110] "Love is the drug, scientists find." *The Telegraph,* July 11, 2014, http://www.telegraph.co.uk/science/science-news/10962885/Love-is-the-drug-scientists-find.html.

[111] Tara Berman, MD, " Sexual Addiction May Be Real After All," *ABC News,* July 11, 2014, http://abcnews.go.com/blogs/health/2014/07/11/sexual-addiction-may-be-real-after-all.

[112] C. Laier, J. Pekal and M. Brand, "Cybersex addiction in heterosexual female users of Internet pornography can be explained by gratification hypothesis" *CyberPsychology, Behavior and Social Networking, CyberPsychology, Behavior and Social Networking* 17/8 (2014): 505-511, doi: 10.1089/cyber.2013.0396.

[113] M. Leyton and P. Vezina, "Striatal ups and downs: their roles in vulnerability to addictions in humans," *Neurosci Biobehav Rev.,* 37/9 (2013): 1999-2014, doi: 10.1016/j.neubiorev.2013.01.018.

[114] Donald L. Hilton, Jr., MD, "Pornography addiction – a supranormal stimulus considered in the context of neuroplasticity," *Socioaffective Neuroscience & Psychology* 3 (2013), http://dx.doi.org/10.3402/snp.v3i0.20767.

[115] Eric J. Nestler, "Is there a common molecular pathway for addiction?" *Nature Neuroscience* 6/11 (2005): 1445-1449, doi:10.1038/nn1578.

[116] N.D. Volkow, "Addiction: decreased reward sensitivity and increased expectation sensitivity conspire to overwhelm the brain's control circuit," *Bioessays* 32/9 (2010): 748-755, doi: 10.1002/bies.201000042.

[117] "Public Policy Statement: Definition of Addiction," *American Association of Addiction Medicine,* April 12, 2011, http://www.asam.org/docs/publicy-policy-statements/1definition_of_addiction_long_4-11.pdf.

[118] Thomas Insel, MD, "Transforming Diagnosis," *National Institute of Mental Health, Director's Blog,* April 29, 2013, http://www.nimh.nih.gov/about/director/2013/transforming-diagnosis.shtml.

[119] Mark Moran, "Gambling Disorder to Be Included in Addictions

Chapter," *Psychiatric News,* April 19, 2013, doi: 10.1176/appi.pn.2013.4b14.

[120] Haifeng Hou, *et al.,* "Reduced Striatal Dopamine Transporters in People with Internet Addiction Disorder," *Journal of Biomedicine and Biotechnology* (2012), Article ID 854524, 5 pages, doi:10.1155/2012/854524.

[121] S.H. Kim *et al.,* "Reduced striatal dopamine D2 receptors in people with Internet addiction," *Neuroreport* 22/8 (2011): 407-411, doi: 10.1097/WNR.0b013e328346e16e.

[122] Jim Rosack, "Volkow May Have Uncovered Answer to Addiction Riddle," *Psychiatric News,* June 4, 2004, http://psychnews.psychiatryonline.org/newsarticle.aspx?articleid=107597.

[123] G. Dong, J. Huang, A. Du, "Enhanced reward sensitivity and decreased loss sensitivity in Internet addicts: an fMRI study during a guessing task," *J Psychiatr Res* 45/11 (2011): 1525-1529. doi: 0.1016/j.jpsychires.2011.06.017.

[124] Adam Withnall, "Pornography addiction leads to same brain activity as alcoholism or drug abuse, study shows," *The Independent,* September 22, 2013, http://www.independent.co.uk/life-style/health-and-families/health-news/pornography-addiction-leads-to-same-brain-activity-as-alcoholism-or-drug-abuse-study-shows-8832708.html.

[125] Kai Yuan, *et al.,* "Microstructure Abnormalities in Adolescents with Internet Addiction Disorder," *PLoS One,* June 03, 2011, doi: 10.1371/journal.pone.0020708.

[126] Y. Zhou, *et al.,* "Grey matter abnormalities in Internet addiction: a voxel-based morphometry study," *Eur J Radiol* 9/1 (2011): 92-95. doi: 10.1016/j.ejrad.2009.10.025.

[127] Fuchun Lin, *et al.,* "Abnormal White Matter Integrity in Adolescents with Internet Addiction Disorder: A Tract-Based Spatial Statistics Study," *PLoS One,* January 11, 2012, doi: 10.1371/journal.pone.0030253.

[128] G. Dong, H. Zhou, X. Zhao, "Impulse inhibition in people with Internet addiction disorder: electrophysiological evidence from a Go/NoGo study," *Neurosci Lett* 485/2 (2010): 138-142, doi: 10.1016/j.neulet.2010.09.002.

[129] G. Dong, H. Zhou, X Zhao, "Male Internet addicts show impaired executive control ability: evidence from a color-word Stroop task," *Neurosci Lett* 499/2 (2011): 114-118, doi: 10.1016/j.neulet.2011.05.047.

[130] Matthias Brand, Kimberly S. Young and Christian Laier, " Prefrontal control and Internet addiction: a theoretical model and review of neuropsychological and neuroimaging findings," *Frontiers in Human Neuroscience* 8/375 (2014), doi: 10.3389/fnhum.2014.00375.

[131] Leigh MacMillan, "Reward-stress link points to new addiction targets,"

Reporter, January 9, 2009, http://www.mc.vanderbilt.edu/reporter/index.html?ID=6916.

[132] Philip J. Hilts, "Is Nicotine Addictive? It Depends on Whose Criteria You Use. Experts say the definition of addiction is evolving," *New York Times,* Aug. 2, 1994, http://www.drugsense.org/tfy/addictvn.htm.

[133] Michela Romano, Lisa A. Osborne, Roberto Truzoli, Phil Reed, "Differential Psychological Impact of Internet Exposure on Internet Addicts," *PLoS One* 8/2 (2013), doi: 10.1371/journal.pone.0055162.

[134] "Web addicts' withdrawal symptoms similar to drug users," *BBC News Wales,* June 19, 2013, http://www.bbc.com/news/uk-wales-22966536.

[135] G.F. Koob, M. Le Moal, "Addiction and the brain antireward system," *Annu Rev Psychol* 59 (2008): 29-53.

[136] David Belin and Aude Rauscent, "DeltaFosB: A Molecular Gate to Motivational Processes within the Nucleus Accumbens?" *The Journal of Neuroscience* 26/46 (2006): 11809–11810.

[137] A.M. Christiansen, A.D. Dekloet, Y.M. Ulrich-Lai, J.P. Herman, "'Snacking' causes long term attenuation of HPA axis stress responses and enhancement of brain FosB/deltaFosB expression in rats," *Physiol Behav* 103/1 (2011): 111-6, doi: 10.1016/j.physbeh.2011.01.015.

[138] V.L. Hedges, S. Chakravarty, E.J. Nestler, and R.L. Meisel, " DeltaFosB overexpression in the nucleus accumbens enhances sexual reward in female Syrian hamsters," *Genes Brain Behav,* 8/4 (2009): 442-449, doi: 10.1111/j.1601-183X.2009.00491.x.

[139] Jennifer Riemersma and Michael Stysma, "A New Generation of Sexual Addiction," *Sexual Addiction & Compulsivity* 20/4 (2013): 306-322, doi: 10.1080/10720162.2013.843067.

[140] J.P. Doucet, *et al.,* "Chronic alterations in dopaminergic neurotransmission produce a persistent elevation of deltaFosB-like protein(s) in both the rodent and primate striatum," *Eur J Neurosci* 8/2 (1996): 365-381.

[141] Eric J. Nestler, Michel Barrot, and David W. Self, "DeltaFosB: A sustained molecular switch for addiction," *PNAS* 98/2 (2001): 11042–11046, doi: 10.1073/pnas.191352698.

[142] Deanna L. Wallace, *et al.,* "The Influence of DeltaFosB in the Nucleus Accumbens on Natural Reward-Related Behavior," *The Journal of Neuroscience* 28/41 (2008): 10272-10277, doi: 10.1523/JNEUROSCI.1531-08.2008.

[143] Kyle K. Pitchers, *et al.,* "DeltaFosB in the nucleus accumbens is critical for reinforcing effects of sexual reward," *Genes Brain Behav* 9/7 (2010): 831-840, doi: 10.1111/j.1601-183X.2010.00621.x.

[144] Deanna L. Wallace, *et al.,* "The Influence of ?FosB in the Nucleus Accumbens on Natural Reward-Related Behavior," *The Journal of Neuroscience* 28/41 (2008): 10272-10277; doi: 10.1523/JNEUROSCI.1531-08.2008.

[145] S.L. Teegarden, E. J. Nestler, T.L. Bale, "DeltaFosB-mediated alterations in dopamine signaling are normalized by a palatable high-fat diet," *Biol Psychiatry* 64/11 (2008): 941-950, doi: 10.1016/j.biopsych.2008.06.007.

[146] Martin Werme *et al.,* "DeltaFosB Regulates Wheel Running," *The Journal of Neuroscience* 22/18 (2002): 8133-8138.

[147] Eric J. Nestler, "Transcriptional mechanisms of addiction: role of ΔFosB," *Phil. Trans. R. Soc. B* 363/1507 (2008): 3245-3255, doi: 10.1098/rstb.2008.0067.

[148] Y. Goto, S. Otani, A.A. Grace, "The Yin and Yang of dopamine release: a new perspective," *Neuropharmacology* 53/5 (2007): 583-587.

[149] Hannah Hames and Sean O'Shea, "Porn causing erectile dysfunction in young men," *Global News,* March 30, 2014, http://globalnews.ca/news/1232726/porn-causing-erectile-dysfunction-in-young-men.

[150] Elizabeth E. Steinberg *et al.,* "A causal link between prediction errors, dopamine neurons and learning," *Nature Neuroscience* 16 (2013): 966–973, doi:10.1038/nn.3413.

[151] Adriana Galvan, *et al.,* "Earlier Development of the Accumbens Relative to Orbitofrontal Cortex Might Underlie Risk-Taking Behavior in Adolescents," *Journal of Neuroscience* 26/25 (2006): 6885-6892, doi: 10.1523/JNEUROSCI.1062-06.2006.

[152] University of Pittsburg, "Teen brains over-process rewards, suggesting root of risky behavior, mental ills," *Phys.org,* January 6, 2011, http://phys.org/news/2011-01-teen-brains-over-process-rewards-root.html.

[153] Eric J. Nestler, "Transcriptional mechanisms of addiction: role of DeltaFosB," *Philosophical Transactions of the Royal Society B* 363/1507 (2008): 3245-3255, doi: 10.1098/rstb.2008.0067.

[154] B.J. Casey and R.M. Jones, "Neurobiology of the adolescent brain and behavior: implications for substance use disorders," *J Am Acad Child Adolesc Psychiatry* 49/12 (2010): 1189-1201, doi: 10.1016/j.jaac.2010.08.017.

[155] C.L. Sisk and J. L. Zehr, "Pubertal hormones organize the adolescent brain and behavior," *Front Neuroendocrinol* 26/3-4 (2005): 163-174.

[156] Tamara L. Doremus-Fitzwater, Elena I. Varlinskaya, Linda P. Spear, "Motivational systems in adolescence: Possible implications for age differences in substance abuse and other risk-taking behaviors," *Brain Cogn* 72/1 (2010): 114-123, doi: 10.1016/j.bandc.2009.08.008.

[157] Candice L. Odgers, "Is It Important to Prevent Early Exposure to Drugs and Alcohol Among Adolescents?" *Psychological Science,* 19/10 (2008): 1037-1044, doi: 10.1111/j.1467-9280.2008.02196.x.

[158] Lawrence T. Lam and Zi-Wen Peng, "Effect of Pathological Use of the Internet on Adolescent Mental Health: A Prospective Study," *Arch Pediatr Adolesc Med* 164/10 (2010): 901-906, doi:10.1001/archpediatrics.2010.159.

[159] Guangheng Dong, Qilin Lu, Hui Zhou and Xuan Zhao, "Precursor or Sequela: Pathological Disorders in People with Internet Addiction Disorder," (2011) DOI: 10.1371/journal.pone.0014703.

[160] I. H. Lin, *et al.,* "The association between suicidality and Internet addiction and activities in Taiwanese adolescents," *Compr Psychiatry* 55/3 (2014): 504-510, doi: 10.1016/j.comppsych.2013.11.012.

[161] A. C. Huang, H. E. Chen, Y. C. Wang, L. M. Wang, "Internet abusers associate with a depressive state but not a depressive trait," 68/3 (2014): 197-205, doi: 10.1111/pcn.12124.

[162] C.H. Ko, *et al.,* "The exacerbation of depression, hostility, and social anxiety in the course of Internet addiction among adolescents: A prospective study" *Compr Psychiatry* (2014) doi: 10.1016/j.comppsych.2014.05.003.

[163] Ine Beyers, Laura Vandebosch and Steven Eggermont, "Early Adolescent Boys' exposure to Internet pornography: Relationships to pubertal timing, sensation seeking, and academic performance" *Journal of Early Adolescence* (in press), https://lirias.kuleuven.be/handle/123456789/458526.

[164] F. Giuliano, J. Allard, "Dopamine and male sexual function," *Eur Urol* 40/6 (2001): 601-608.

[165] M.R. Melis, A. Argiolas, "Central control of penile erection: a re-visitation of the role of oxytocin and its interaction with dopamine and glutamic acid in male rats," *Neurosci Biobehav Rev* 35/3 (2011): 939-955. doi: 10.1016/j.neubiorev.2010.10.014.

[166] N. Cera, *et al.,* "Macrostructural alterations of subcortical grey matter in psychogenic erectile dysfunction," *PLoS One* 7/6, (2012), doi: 10.1371/journal.pone.0039118.

[167] Simone Kühn and Jürgen Gallinat, "Brain Structure and Functional Connectivity Associated With Pornography Consumption: The Brain on Porn," *JAMA Psychiatry* (2014), doi:10.1001/jamapsychiatry.2014.93.

[168] Kyle K. Pitchers, *et al.,* "DeltaFosB in the nucleus accumbens is critical for reinforcing effects of sexual reward," *Genes Brain Behav* 9/7 (2010): 831-840, doi: 10.1111/j.1601-183X.2010.00621.x.

[169] Elaine M. Hull, "Sex, Drugs and Gluttony: How the Brain Controls Motivated Behaviors," *Physiol Behav* 104(1) (2011): 173-177, doi: 10.1016/j.physbeh.2011.04.057.

[170] A. R. Oliveira, *et al.*, "Conditioned fear is modulated by D2 receptor pathway connecting the ventral tegmental area and basolateral amygdala," 95(1) (2011): 37-45, doi: 10.1016/j.nlm.2010.10.005.

[171] Marijke Vroomen Durning, "PET Scans Link Low Dopamine Levels and Aggression," *Diagnostic Imaging*, June 12, 2012, http://www.diagnosticimaging.com/nuclear-imaging/pet-scans-link-low-dopamine-levels-and-aggression.

[172] Nora D. Volkow, *et al.*, "Evaluating Dopamine Reward Pathway in ADHD," *JAMA* 302(10) 2010: 1084-1091, doi: 10.1001/jama.2009.1308.

[173] P. Trifilieff, *et al.*, "Increasing dopamine D2 receptor expression in the adult nucleus accumbens enhances motivation," *Mol Psychiatry* 18(9) (2013): 1025-1033, doi: 10.1038/mp.2013.57.

[174] N. D. Volkow, *et al.*, "Motivation deficit in ADHD is associated with dysfunction of the dopamine reward pathway," *Mol Psychiatry* 16(11) (2011): 1147-1154, doi: 10.1038/mp.2010.97.

[175] Donald S. Robinson, "The Role of Dopamine and Norepinephrine in Depression," *Primary Psychiatry*, May 1, 2007, http://primarypsychiatry.com/the-role-of-dopamine-and-norepinephrine-in-depression.

[176] Lieuwe de Haan, *et al.*, "Subjective Experiences During Dopamine Depletion," *The American Journal of Psychiatry* 162 (2005):1755-1755, doi:10.1176/appi.ajp.162.9.1755.

[177] S. H. Kim *et al.*, "Reduced striatal dopamine D2 receptors in people with Internet addiction," *Neuroreport* 22(8) (2011): 407-411, doi: 10.1097/WNR.0b013e328346e16e.

[178] Paul M. Johnson and Paul Kenny, *Nat Neurosci* 13(5) (2010): 653-641, doi: 10.1038/nn.2519
PMCID: PMC2947358.

[179] Eric Stice, Sonja Yokum, Kenneth Blum and Cara Bohon, "Weight Gain Is Associated with Reduced Striatal Response to Palatable Food," *The Journal of Neuroscience*, 30/39 (2010): 13105-13109, doi: 10.1523/JNEUROSCI.2105-10.2010.

[180] Magdalena Mattebo et al., "Pornography consumption, psychosomatic health and depressive symptoms among Swedish adolescents" *Digitala Vetenskapliga Arkivet,*(2014), http://www.diva-portal.org/smash/record.

[181] David J. Ley, "An Erectile Dysfunction Myth," *Psychology Today* Blogs,

August 29, 2013, http://www.psychologytoday.com/blog/women-who-stray/201308/erectile-dysfunction-myth.

[182] Wayland Hsiao, *et al.,* "Exercise is Associated with Better Erectile Function in Men Under 40 as Evaluated by the International Index of Erectile Function," *The Journal of Sexual Medicine* 9/2 (2012): 524-530, doi: 10.1111/j.1743-6109.2011.02560.x.

[183] P.G. MacRae, W.W. Spirduso, G..D. Cartee, R.P. Farrar and R.E. Wilcox, "Endurance training effects on striatal D2 dopamine receptor binding and striatal dopamine metabolite levels," *Neurosci Lett* 79/1-2 (1987): 138-144.

[184] M.A. Smith, K.T. Schmidt, J.C. Iordanou and M.L. Mustroph "Aerobic exercise decreases the positive-reinforcing effects of cocaine," *Drug Alcohol Depend* 98/1-2 (2008): 129-135, doi: 10.1016/j.drugalcdep.2008.05.006.

[185] N.A Shevchuk, "Adapted cold shower as a potential treatment for depression," *Med Hypotheses* 70/5 (2008): 995-1001.

[186] Brendan Lynch, "Researchers find time in wild boosts creativity, insight and problem solving," The University of Kansas, April 23, 2012, http://archive.news.ku.edu/2012/april/23/outdoors.shtml.

[187] "Study shows tranquil scenes have positive impact on brain," The University of Sheffield, September 14, 2010, http://www.sheffield.ac.uk/news/nr/1739-1.174080.

[188] Tara Parker-Pope, "Is Marriage Good For Your Health?" *The New York Times,* April 14, 2010, http://www.nytimes.com/2010/04/18/magazine/18marriage-t.html?pagewanted=all&_r=0.

[189] E. Luders, A.W. Toga, N. Lepore and C. Gaser, "The underlying anatomical correlates of long-term meditation: larger hippocampal and frontal volumes of gray matter," *Neuroimage,*45/3 (2009): 672-678.

[190] N.M. Avena and P.V. Rada, "Cholinergic modulation of food and drug satiety and withdrawal," *Physiol Behav* 106/3 (2012): 332-336, doi: 10.1016/j.physbeh.2012.03.020.

[191] R.B. Kanarek, K.E. D'Anci, N. Jurak and W.F. Mathes, "Running and addiction: precipitated withdrawal in a rat model of activity-based anorexia," *Behav Neurosci,* 123/4 (2009) 905-912, doi: 10.1037/a0015896.

[192] S. Sharma, M.F. Fernandes and S. Fulton, "Adaptations in brain reward circuitry underlie palatable food cravings and anxiety induced by high-fat diet withdrawal," *Int J Obes (Lond)* 37/9 (2013): 1183-1191, doi: 10.1038/ijo.2012.197.

[193] "How I Recovered from Porn-related Erectile Dysfunction," *Your Brain*

On Porn, http://yourbrainonporn.com/how-i-recovered-from-porn-related-erectile-dysfunction.

[194] Wynne K. Schiffer, *et al.*, "Cue-Induced Dopamine Release Predicts Cocaine Preference: Positron Emission Tomography Studies in Freely Moving Rodents," *The Journal of Neuroscience* 29/19 (2009): 6176–6185.

[195] David H.Barlow, David K. Sakheim, J. Gayle Beck, "Anxiety increases sexual arousal," *Journal of Abnormal Psychology* 92/1 (1983): 49-54.

[196] "Why does vivid memory 'feel so real?' Real perceptual experience, mental replay share similar brain activation patterns," *Medical Express,* July 23, 2012, http://medicalxpress.com/news/2012-07-vivid-memory-real-perceptual-mental.html.

[197] Frederick Toates, *How Sexual Desire Works: The Enigmatic Urge,* Cambridge: Cambridge University Press, (2014): 335.

[198] Kathryn C. Seigfried-Spellar and Marcus K. Rogers, "Does deviant pornography use follow a Guttman-like progression?" *Computers in Human Behavior* 29/5 (2013): 1997–2003, http://dx.doi.org/10.1016/j.chb.2013.04.018.

[199] NoFap Survey results, *http://www.reddit.com/r/NoFap*, April 2012, https://docs.google.com/file/d/0B7q3tr4EV02wbkpTTVk4R2VGbm8/edit?pli=1.

[200] "Looking at porn on the internet could ruin your sex life, doctor says," *Metro*, April 16, 2014, http://metro.co.uk/2014/04/16/looking-at-porn-on-the-internet-could-ruin-your-sex-life-doctor-says-4700884.

[201] "Your Brain In The Cybersex Jungle" radio show, *KSKQ*, February 10, 2014, www.archive.org audio file: http://ia600900.us.archive.org/15/items/Cyber20130716/cyber20130716.mp3.

[202] P. Capogrosso, *et al.* "One patient out of four with newly diagnosed erectile dysfunction is a young man--worrisome picture from the everyday clinical practice," *J Sex Med* 10/7 (2013): 1833-1841, doi: 10.1111/jsm.12179.

[203] Lucia F. O'Sullivan, *et al.*, "Prevalence and Characteristics of Sexual Functioning among Sexually Experienced Middle to Late Adolescents," *J Sex Med* 11/3 (2014): 630-641, doi: 10.1111/jsm.12419.

[204] S.L. Wilcox, S. Redmond and A.M. Hassan, "Sexual Functioning in Military Personnel: Preliminary Estimates and Predictors," *J Sex Med* (2014) doi: 10.1111/jsm.12643. [Epub ahead of print].

[205] "Can Porn Cause Erectile Dysfunction?" *Dr. Oz Show* (TV), January 31, 2013, http://www.doctoroz.com/videos/can-porn-cause-erectile-dysfunction-pt-1.

[206] Simone Kühn and Jürgen Gallinat, "Brain Structure and Functional Connectivity Associated With Pornography Consumption: The Brain on Porn," *JAMA Psychiatry* (2014), doi:10.1001/jamapsychiatry.2014.93.

[207] Valerie Voon, *et al.,* "Neural Correlates of Sexual Cue Reactivity in Individuals with and without Compulsive Sexual Behaviours", *PLOS One* (2014): DOI: 10.1371/journal.pone.0102419.

[208] A. Bailin, R. Milanaik, and A. Adesman, "Health implications of new age technologies for adolescents: a review of the research," *Curr Opin Pediatr.* 26/5 (2014): 605-19, doi: 10.1097/MOP.0000000000000140.

[209] Owens, Eric W. et al., "The Impact of Internet Pornography on Adolescents: A Review of the Research." *Sexual Addiction & Compulsivity,* 19/1-2 (2012): 99-122, http://dx.doi.org/10.1080/10720162.2012.660431..

[210] G.M. Hald, N.M. Malamuth C. Yuen, "Pornography and attitudes supporting violence against women: revisiting the relationship in nonexperimental studies," *Aggress Behav* 36/1 (2010): 14-20, doi: 10.1002/ab.20328.

[211] Linda Hatch, PhD, "The Bogus Sex Addiction 'Controversy' and the Purveyors of Ignorance," *PsychCentral,* March, 2014, http://blogs.psychcentral.com/sex-addiction/2014/03/the-bogus-porn-addiction-controversy-and-the-purveyors-of-ignorance.

[212] T.M. Zhu, *et al.,* "Effects of electroacupuncture combined psycho-intervention on cognitive function and event-related potentials P300 and mismatch negativity in patients with internet addiction," *Chin J Integr Med* 18/2 (2012): 146-151, doi: 10.1007/s11655-012-0990-5.

[213] Simone Kühn and Jürgen Gallinat, "Brain Structure and Functional Connectivity Associated With Pornography Consumption: The Brain on Porn," *JAMA Psychiatry* (2014), doi:10.1001/jamapsychiatry.2014.93.

[214] Valerie Voon, *et al.,* "Neural Correlates of Sexual Cue Reactivity in Individuals with and without Compulsive Sexual Behaviours", *PLOS One* (2014): DOI: 10.1371/journal.pone.0102419.

[215] Porn Study Critiques, "Pornography Consumption Effect Scale: Useful or Not?" (2013), http://pornstudycritiques.com/self-perceived-effects-of-pornography-consumption-2008-hald-gm-malamuth-nm.

[216] C. Marston and R. Lewis, "Anal heterosex among young people and implications for health promotion: a qualitative study in the UK," (2014), doi:10.1136/bmjopen-2014-004996.

[217] Simone Kühn and Jürgen Gallinat, "Brain Structure and Functional Connectivity Associated With Pornography Consumption: The Brain on Porn," *JAMA Psychiatry* (2014), doi:10.1001/jamapsychiatry.2014.93.

[218] Institute for Public Policy Research, "500 Online Interviews amongst UK adults aged 18, Field 19th to 27th June 2014" http://www.ippr.org/publications/young-people-sex-and-relationships-the-new-norms.